**New Directions for
Teaching and Learning**

Catherine M. Wehlburg
EDITOR-IN-CHIEF

The Scholarship of Teaching and Learning in Canada: Institutional Impact

Nicola Simmons

EDITOR

Number 146 • Summer 2016
Jossey-Bass
San Francisco

THE SCHOLARSHIP OF TEACHING AND LEARNING IN CANADA: INSTITUTIONAL IMPACT
Nicola Simmons (ed.)
New Directions for Teaching and Learning, no. 146
Catherine M. Wehlburg, Editor-in-Chief

Microfilm copies of issues and articles are available in 16 mm and 35 mm, as well as microfiche in 105 mm, through University Microfilms, Inc., 300 North Zeeb Road, Ann Arbor, MI 48106-1346.

NEW DIRECTIONS FOR TEACHING AND LEARNING (ISSN 0271-0633, electronic ISSN 1536-0768) is part of The Jossey-Bass Higher and Adult Education Series and is published quarterly by Wiley Subscription Services, Inc., A Wiley Company, at Jossey-Bass, One Montgomery Street, Suite 1200, San Francisco, CA 94104-4594. POSTMASTER: Send address changes to New Directions for Teaching and Learning, Jossey-Bass, One Montgomery Street, Suite 1200, San Francisco, CA 94104-4594.

New Directions for Teaching and Learning is indexed in CIJE: Current Index to Journals in Education (ERIC), Contents Pages in Education (T&F), Educational Research Abstracts Online (T&F), ERIC Database (Education Resources Information Center), Higher Education Abstracts (Claremont Graduate University), and SCOPUS (Elsevier).

INDIVIDUAL SUBSCRIPTION RATE (in USD): $89 per year US/Can/Mex, $113 rest of world; institutional subscription rate: $335 US, $375 Can/Mex, $409 rest of world. Single copy rate: $29. Electronic only–all regions: $89 individual, $335 institutional; Print & Electronic–US: $98 individual, $402 institutional; Print & Electronic–Can/Mex: $98 individual, $442 institutional; Print & Electronic–rest of world: $122 individual, $476 institutional.

Cover design: Wiley
Cover Images: © Lava 4 images | Shutterstock

EDITORIAL CORRESPONDENCE should be sent to the editor-in-chief, Catherine M. Wehlburg, c.wehlburg@tcu.edu.

www.josseybass.com

CONTENTS

EDITOR'S NOTES   7
Nicola Simmons

FOREWORD   11
Nancy Chick

Section One: Canadian Context

1. The History of SoTL in Canada: Answering Calls for Action   13
Nicola Simmons, Gary Poole
This chapter provides an account of the historical development of SoTL
in Canada, including recommendations for moving forward.

2. The Canadian Teaching Commons: The Scholarship of   23
Teaching and Learning in Canadian Higher Education
Brad Wuetheric, Stan Yu
This chapter maps the Scholarship of Teaching and Learning (SoTL)
terrain in Canada through the perceptions of SoTL scholars at four
levels (micro, meso, macro, mega).

Section Two: Program Design And Evaluation

3. The Intentional Design of a SoTL Initiative   31
Cheryl Amundsen, Esma Emmioglu, Veronica Hotton, Gregory Hum,
Cindy Xin
This chapter outlines how rationale and description of a program
design are the underpinnings to evaluate any Scholarship of Teaching
and Learning initiative and shows how this supports building on prior
practice.

4. The Scholarship of Teaching and Learning (SoTL) at   39
Renaissance College (University of New Brunswick): A Case
Study of SoTL at the Faculty Level
Thomas Mengel
This chapter discusses how a university college moves SoTL forward
by aligning with the larger institution and taking advantage of SoTL-
friendly existing promotion and tenure policies.

5. Developing the Scholarship of Teaching and Learning at the   47
McMaster Institute for Innovation and Excellence in Teaching
and Learning
Elizabeth Marquis, Arshad Ahmad
This chapter outlines how research fellow positions, engagement of students as co-inquirers, and mapping priority areas for scholarship have the potential for substantial impact on institutional teaching, learning, and SOTL.

Section Three: Exploring the Impact of SoTL Initiatives

6. SoTL^2: Inquiring into the Impact of Inquiry   55
Janice Miller-Young, Michelle Yeo, Karen Manarin, Miriam Carey,
Jim Zimmer
This chapter examines the impact of Mount Royal's SoTL program on participants' scholarship at individual, department, and institutional levels as the institution moved from a college to a university.

7. Exploring the SoTL Landscape at the University of   63
Saskatchewan
Brad Wuetherick, Stan Yu, Jim Greer
This chapter examines who conducts Scholarship of Teaching and Learning, and to what extent, at the University of Saskatchewan and what barriers and challenges impede SoTL work.

8. Reconceptualizing the Scholarship of Teaching and Learning   71
at the University of Waterloo: An Account of Influences and
Impact
Julie A. Timmermans, Donna E. Ellis
This chapter outlines how one institution capitalized on events to move from a focus on SoTL to scholarly teaching and discusses the resulting benefits to the culture of teaching and learning.

Section Four: Institutionally Networked SoTL

9. The Role of Small Significant Networks and Leadership in   79
the Institutional Embedding of SoTL
Roselynn Verwoord, Gary Poole
This chapter builds on notions of social networks, showing how consideration of their nature, relationships between them, and support for them can help create a positive teaching culture.

10. Building Sustained Action: Supporting an Institutional   87
Practice of SoTL at the University of Guelph
Natasha Kenny, Gavan P.L. Watson, Serge Desmarais
This chapter outlines the symbiotic relationship between engagement in SoTL and a teaching-focused institutional culture, identifying the importance of committed leaders, rewards and recognition, and integrated networks at all organizational levels.

Section Five: Synthesis

11. Synthesizing SoTL Institutional Initiatives toward National   95
Impact

Nicola Simmons
This chapter draws together the themes in this issue and outlines
a model for building from institutional SoTL impact to national
initiatives.

INDEX   103

FROM THE SERIES EDITOR

About This Publication

Since 1980, *New Directions for Teaching and Learning* (NDTL) has brought a unique blend of theory, research, and practice to leaders in postsecondary education. NDTL sourcebooks strive not only for solid substance but also for timeliness, compactness, and accessibility.

The series has four goals: (1) to inform readers about current and future directions in teaching and learning in postsecondary education, (2) to illuminate the context that shapes these new directions, (3) to illustrate these new directions through examples from real settings, and (4) to propose ways in which these new directions can be incorporated into still other settings.

This publication reflects the view that teaching deserves respect as a high form of scholarship. We believe that significant scholarship is conducted not only by researchers who report results of empirical investigations but also by practitioners who share disciplinary reflections about teaching. Contributors to NDTL approach questions of teaching and learning as seriously as they approach substantive questions in their own disciplines, and they deal not only with pedagogical issues but also with the intellectual and social contexts in which these issues arise. Authors deal, on the one hand, with theory and research and, on the other, with practice, and they translate from research and theory to practice and back again.

About This Volume

This volume focuses on the ways that higher education institutions in Canada have worked to develop and continue programs for the Scholarship of Teaching and Learning (SoTL). Each chapter provides information about effective SoTL models and the impact that these models have on teaching and, ultimately, student learning. As many have seen, the growth of SoTL programs has had incredibly positive outcomes for pedagogy and for improving and enhancing student learning. By providing these scholarly examples of teaching and learning, this volume gives readers the opportunity to learn about how to incorporate aspects of SoTL into institutional initiatives to improve teaching and learning.

Catherine M. Wehlburg
Editor in Chief

CATHERINE M. WEHLBURG is the associate provost for institutional effectiveness at Texas Christian University.

EDITOR'S NOTES

The Scholarship of Teaching and Learning (SoTL) is a growing area in which postsecondary educators from any discipline investigate their teaching and their students' learning, sharing those results with others. As McKinney (2006, 3) notes, SoTL "involves systematic study of teaching and/or learning and the public sharing and review of such work through presentations, performance, or publications." This work thus informs scholarly teaching practice, and for some who make it public beyond their classrooms, it also builds pedagogical knowledge in and across the disciplines.

In the Canadian context, Poole, Taylor, and Thompson (2007) discussed how using scholarship of teaching and learning at various levels (institutional, disciplinary, and national) could improve postsecondary educational quality, but little work has been done to assess to what extent their recommendations have been implemented. Wutherick and Yu's chapter mapping SoTL activities in Canada makes it is clear that much SoTL is happening across the country, and in many institutions, this work is supported by grants, staff, and collaborative research groups. So far there is little evidence, however, of the impact of SoTL on teaching and learning quality at the institutional level. As Christensen Hughes and Mighty (2010, 4) have noted, "researchers have discovered much about teaching and learning in higher education, but ... dissemination and uptake of this information have been limited. As such, the impact of educational research on faculty-teaching practice and the student-learning experience has been negligible." More recently, Poole and Simmons (2013) have identified the continuing need for assessing SoTL's impact on institutional quality.

The purpose of this special issue is to provide examples and evidence of the ways in which postsecondary institutions in Canada have developed and sustained programs around the Scholarship of Teaching and Learning that impact the institutional pedagogical climate. The various chapters outline practices, include evidence of impact, and discuss continuing challenges with this work. Our hope is to thus conceptualize the work of SoTL

NEW DIRECTIONS FOR TEACHING AND LEARNING, no. 146, Summer 2016 © 2016 Wiley Periodicals, Inc.
Published online in Wiley Online Library (wileyonlinelibrary.com) • DOI: 10.1002/tl.20180

and provide enough detail so that others may develop effective models of practice.

Canadian Context

Chapter 1, by Simmons and Poole, provides an overview of the Canadian postsecondary context, including the political structure for higher education (necessary for understanding the particular challenges in securing resources for SoTL both internal to the institution and from external sources), the types of postsecondary institutions, and a brief overview of SoTL history in Canada, including national and provincial organizations.

In Chapter 2, Wuetherick and Yu describe findings from a national survey of the professional life of SoTL scholars. Using the micro-meso-macro-mega framework, they examine the SoTL organizational culture in Canada and note how alignment of these levels helps move the SoTL forward. They advocate for leaders to champion the SoTL cause in order to advance SoTL from the micro to the mega levels.

Case Studies

Subsequent chapters present case studies from different postsecondary institutions across Canada and are organized in three sections: Program Design and Evaluation, Exploring the Impact of SoTL Initiatives, and Institutionally Networked SoTL. These sections outline the design and impact of SoTL initiatives, including how evidence of institutional impact is being collected, findings to date, and recommendations for future inquiry.

Program Design and Evaluation. In Chapter 3, Amundsen, Emmioglu, Hotton, Hum, and Xin detail the planning of an SoTL program at Simon Fraser University, British Columbia. They describe how analyzing the internal coherence and alignment of the program design and the thinking underpinning the design is the first step in evaluating effectiveness or impact. SoTL is positioned as a socially situated practice, and they note the importance of further investigating the connections amongst the levels.

In Chapter 4, Mengel describes how Rennaissance College moved SoTL forward by aligning with the larger institution's promotion and tenure policies that recognize SoTL as equivalent to disciplinary research. Mengel outlines challenges that face many institutions, such as how to keep SoTL momentum in fiscally challenging times. He argues that SoTL will only be sustainable if it is strongly anchored in the strategic plan of the faculties and the vision of their members.

Chapter 5, by Marquis and Ahmad, outlines the development of McMaster University's new SoTL institute and how that has positively supported SoTL growth on campus. Their case study presentation also highlights that support for those already moving SoTL forward to join like-minded others can multiply the impact. They also discuss how leaders can support student involvement in SoTL and they emphasize the value of aligning SoTL with institutional priorities.

Exploring the Impact of SoTL Initiatives.   In Chapter 6, Miller-Young, Yeo, Manarin, Carey, and Zimmer outline perceptions of participants in their Nexen Scholars program. They note that high-level institutional support for SoTL has been critical to the institute's success. Their findings revealed a development in SoTL scholars' perceptions of the impact of their work: Newcomers are more likely to frame the impact in individual terms, whereas more experienced SoTL scholars are more likely to consider the departmental, institutional, and disciplinary impacts.

In Chapter 7, Wuetherick, Yu, and Greer outline results of a survey of SoTL at the University of Saskatchewan. Their participants note the challenges of lack of legitimacy (SoTL is not currently tied to promotion and tenure) and time, and these are tied to how SoTL work is seen within academic departments. They also note there are discernible shifts in the culture toward being more amenable to SoTL work.

In Chapter 8, Timmermans and Ellis examine the role of the teaching and learning center in supporting SoTL and describe the shift, catalyzed by change in staff at the center, from focusing on traditionally defined SoTL toward scholarly teaching, which they found to be more inclusive of the kind of work being done on campus. They advocate an approach to SoTL that draws on the principles of starting where people are and knowing and adapting to the institutional context.

Institutionally Networked SoTL.   Chapter 9, by Verwoord and Poole (University of British Columbia), focuses on how social networks of individuals can build toward an institutional movement. They provide examples of how these local networks form, how appointed leaders could identify and support them, and also how junior colleagues can benefit from being part of these networks. They advocate for paying attention to multilevel social networks, including how they form and how they can be sustained toward greater institutional SoTL impact.

In Chapter 10, Kenny, Watson, and Desmarais discuss the cultural shift that occurred as the University of Guelph placed a higher emphasis on the value of teaching and learning. They highlight the role of senior administration in clearly communicating their vision and the process needed to achieve it and in providing necessary resources for quality enhancement. They emphasize the importance of meso- or department-level supports such as community of practice networks, department-specific funding, and inclusion of graduate students in SoTL work.

Synthesis

The volume ends with Chapter 11, in which Simmons discusses what can be learned from the case studies as a group, drawing parallels and exploring

NEW DIRECTIONS FOR TEACHING AND LEARNING • DOI: 10.1002/tl

distinctions and ultimately mapping recommendations for a synthesized model for creating a national context for SoTL's growth.

Nicola Simmons

References

Christensen Hughes, Julia, and Joy Mighty. 2010. *Taking Stock: Research on Teaching and Learning*. Montreal, QC and Kingston, ON: McGill-Queen's University Press.

McKinney, Kathleen. 2006. "Attitudinal and Structural Factors Contributing to Challenges in the Work of the Scholarship of Teaching and Learning." *New Directions for Institutional Research* 129(Summer): 37–50.

Poole, Gary, Lynn Taylor, and John Thompson. 2007. "Using the Scholarship of Teaching and Learning at Disciplinary, National and Institutional Levels to Strategically Improve the Quality of Post-secondary Education." *International Journal for the Scholarship of Teaching and Learning* 1(2): Article 3.

Poole, Gary, and Nicola Simmons. 2013. "Contributions of the Scholarship of Teaching and Learning to Quality Enhancement in Canada." In *Enhancing Quality in Higher Education: International Perspectives*, edited by Ray Land and George Gordon, 118–28. London: Routledge.

NICOLA SIMMONS *was the founding chair of SoTL Canada and is currently a faculty member in the faculty of education at Brock University in Ontario.*

NEW DIRECTIONS FOR TEACHING AND LEARNING • DOI: 10.1002/tl

FOREWORD

This volume of *New Directions in Teaching and Learning* documents the varied landscape of the Scholarship of Teaching and Learning (SoTL) in Canada. Each chapter illustrates how involvement with SoTL benefits institutions, colleagues, and students because SoTL tells "the story of teaching," one that revolves around the pursuit of "the best ways to promote deep student learning" (Bernstein 2013, 36–37).

Even in difficult economic times, the following stories resist what O'Meara, Terosky, and Neumann identify in *Faculty Careers and Work Lives* (2008) as the theme of most narratives told from those inside the profession: the theme of "constraint." With language like "'just making it,' 'treading water,' 'dodging bullets,' or barely 'staying alive,'" narratives of constraint describe an environment plagued by barriers, external forces, limitations, and frustration (2). The following pages, however, depict an alternative and less frequently voiced theme in "narratives of growth" (3). These stories present people and places characterized by relationships, enrichment, commitment, agency, and professional fulfillment without ignoring the challenges for those who do, support, and advocate for SoTL (25–26).

This volume belongs on shelves across campus, not just in teaching and learning centers. Administrators and teaching staff will be able to compare their distinct contexts to those described in these pages and learn from others' practices and responses to institutional culture. Students will see the work that's being done—often behind the scenes, from their perspectives—to promote their learning.

This volume belongs on the reading list for a Canadian summit of institutional leaders, who will brainstorm strategies for expanding the sponsorship of SoTL at and between their institutions.

This volume also belongs on the desks of provincial government officials who talk about the importance of higher education but are unaware of

NEW DIRECTIONS FOR TEACHING AND LEARNING, no. 146, Summer 2016 © 2016 Wiley Periodicals, Inc.
Published online in Wiley Online Library (wileyonlinelibrary.com) • DOI: 10.1002/tl.20181

SoTL, the most effective on-the-ground activity that strengthens the work of the university.

It belongs on the to-do lists of other Canadian campuses, so more will share their SoTL stories.

It belongs in a stack of models for other countries to document the specific structures for SoTL (or the lack thereof) around the world.

Finally, this volume belongs in the bibliographies of the international SoTL community as we push ourselves to explore how the particularities of contexts—not just our own—affect the institutions, cultures, and practices of the scholarship of teaching and learning.

Nancy Chick

References

Bernstein, Dan. 2013. "How SoTL-active Faculty Members Can Be Cosmopolitan Assets to an Institution." *Teaching & Learning Inquiry* 1(1): 35–40.

O'Meara, KerryAnn, Aimee LaPointe Terosky, and Anna Neumann. 2008. *Faculty Careers and Work Lives: A Professional Growth Perspective*. San Francisco, CA: Jossey-Bass.

NANCY CHICK *is university chair in teaching and learning; academic director of the Taylor Institute for Teaching and Learning, University of Calgary; and founding co-editor,* Teaching & Learning Inquiry: The ISSOTL Journal.

NEW DIRECTIONS FOR TEACHING AND LEARNING • DOI: 10.1002/tl

1

This chapter outlines the historical growth of the Scholarship of Teaching and Learning (SoTL) in Canada leading up to the formation of SoTL Canada and the development of this volume.

The History of SoTL in Canada: Answering Calls for Action

Nicola Simmons, Gary Poole

In this chapter, we discuss the Canadian context for the growth of the Scholarship of Teaching and Learning (SoTL), noting the structural ways in which that postsecondary education arena differs from that of other countries. We outline some key elements of the history of SoTL's development in Canada, culminating with the formation of SoTL Canada and the publication of this volume. In this chapter, we highlight successful initiatives that have been undertaken and discuss key considerations that still must be addressed in order to see SoTL develop strongly across Canada.

The Origins of the Scholarship of Teaching and Learning

In 1990, in his treatise on the four different types of scholarship that comprise academic work, Boyer introduced the notion of the Scholarship of Teaching, suggesting that teaching that contributed to others' enlightenment was, in and of itself, scholarly work that should be seen as equivalent to the more traditional view of scholarship as disciplinary research. Over the years, *learning* was added to make explicit the focus on student learning. As the Society of Teaching and Learning in Higher Education (STLHE, n.d.) website defines it,

> The Scholarship of Teaching and Learning (SoTL) is an emerging movement of scholarly thought and action that draws on the reciprocal relationship between teaching and learning at the post-secondary level (Boyer, 1990). An important goal of SoTL is to enhance and augment learning amongst and between individual learners by investigating the many features of discipline specific expertise and best pedagogical practice. (McKinney, 2006)

NEW DIRECTIONS FOR TEACHING AND LEARNING, no. 146, Summer 2016 © 2016 Wiley Periodicals, Inc.
Published online in Wiley Online Library (wileyonlinelibrary.com) • DOI: 10.1002/tl.20182

Further, as Poole and Simmons (2013, 118) note:

Hutchings and Shulman (1999) further clarify that SoTL "requires a kind of 'going meta,' in which faculty frame and systematically investigate questions related to student learning" (p. 13). The overall intention of SoTL is thus to improve student learning and enhance educational quality.

While Boyer put forward his notion of the scholarship of teaching in 1990, it took a few years to establish the momentum that became a movement; by the early 2000s, many institutions and even national organizations around the world supported and sometimes funded SoTL work (for example, the Carnegie CASTL program that was launched in the United States in 1998) (Hutchings, Huber, and Ciccone 2011). Early publications and collaborations and a growing sense of excitement for SoTL's potential impact led to the formation of the International Society for the Scholarship of Teaching and Learning (ISSoTL) in 2004 (see www.issotl.com/issotl15/).

The Canadian Context

In Canada, higher education is the responsibility of individual provinces rather than being under national jurisdiction. Poole and Simmons (2013) outlined several challenges that arise from this; for example, while there is national disciplinary research funding in Canada, obtaining similar support for pedagogical research at the postsecondary level, considered to be a provincial responsibility, can be near impossible. Further, they point out that the push for educational quality is also a provincial focus (this is different from other countries, most notably Australia and the United Kingdom). In addition, there are no national databases that would provide significant sample sizes for comparisons in SoTL work. As Poole and Simmons (2013) note, "the nature of SoTL and its context thus vary considerably across the country, making it an oversimplification to discuss Canadian higher education as though it were a homogeneous sector or had discernible national character" (119). The experience of moving SoTL forward in Canada has thus been somewhat different from other contexts.

SoTL in Canada: Early Days

In 2004, concurrently with the ISSoTL's development, the Society for Teaching and Learning in Higher Education (STLHE) (see www.stlhe.ca) identified *Advancing the Scholarship of Teaching and Learning* as the first of its four primary strategic directions, referred to as its *pillars*, each with its own vice president. In the case of SoTL, that first vice president was Harry Hubball, who was tasked with defining SoTL, communicating its importance, and developing a rationale and guidelines for postsecondary institutions. This early work, in combination with that of his successor, Lynn Taylor, herself

NEW DIRECTIONS FOR TEACHING AND LEARNING • DOI: 10.1002/tl

a key responder to national calls for action, led to a number of high impact national initiatives.

For example, in 2005, with the strong support of the STLHE board and past president (2000–2004) Gary Poole and president (2004–2007) Julia Christensen Hughes, Lynn Taylor and Teresa Dawson, on behalf of STLHE, co-organized with the Centre for Higher Education Research and Development the first national Leadership Forum on SoTL, which was held in Ontario. It brought 90 senior university administrators from across Canada together with heads of national funding councils to have conversations about how engaging in SoTL could benefit institutions (Poole 2010). Two significant milestones of this event were the first Canadian keynote by a senior administrator (Anna Kindler, University of British Columbia) on the potential value of SoTL to institutions. It was also the first time that the national Tri-Council Agencies funding agencies were represented on a panel to explore SoTL's potential impact, in this case by Janet Halliwell of the Social Sciences and Humanities Research Council.

Certainly, SoTL was gaining greater recognition, and a number of institutions were developing strong SoTL programs and offering local SoTL conferences (Mount Royal College, University of British Columbia, University of Waterloo, and the University of Western Ontario, to name a few). In October 2005, ISSoTL held its second annual conference in Vancouver, British Columbia, which helped us see that national advocacy was a compelling international issue, and there were discussions around the globe about what kinds of national initiatives would support SoTL work more broadly. It was clear, however, that despite shared goals, the context for SoTL in Canada was not the same as elsewhere. Julia Christensen Hughes (2006), then president of STLHE, presented her own call for action in her reflections on the international panel in which she participated:

> As I listened to my colleagues describe the initiatives that were underway in their own countries, I was struck by the "grass roots" nature of the movement in Canada. In Canada there have been no multi-million dollar SoTL programs, foundations, centres of excellence, or granting councils established for supporting this important work. We also have no government mandated requirements for preparing PhD students or new faculty for their teaching roles or ensuring some minimal level of exposure to the pedagogical literature. (para. 6)

It was clear that Canada's SoTL agenda faced some unique challenges that the Canadian SoTL community would need to address.

In 2006, a group convened to discuss possibilities for a Canadian SoTL agenda. From this, further STLHE board discussions led to a SoTL advisory panel to consider how to best move SoTL forward as a national initiative. The inaugural panel was chaired by Nicola Simmons, at the time STLHE vice president responsible for SoTL, and it met for the first time in 2009.

Initially, the panel discussed what SoTL initiatives were already in place and pointed to the increase in SoTL work at the annual conference, the Educational Developers Caucus small grants for SoTL work, and collaboration with the Higher Education Quality Council of Ontario (HEQCO) to develop an international symposium on teaching and learning. This international symposium led to the Taking Stock Symposium in April 2008 to focus on what was known about student learning and to identify gaps in knowledge and research to date, resulting in the *Taking Stock* book coedited by STLHE past and current presidents Julia Christensen Hughes and Joy Mighty. The key message resulting from this conference was that there is an unacceptable gap between what is known through research and what is implemented in postsecondary teaching practices. As Christensen Hughes and Mighty (2010, 4) noted in the book, "researchers have discovered much about teaching and learning in higher education, but ... dissemination and uptake of this information have been limited." This was a serious call to action for SoTL work.

During this time, other efforts by the SoTL advisory panel included providing input to the Canadian Tri-Council's guidelines for research ethics (Simmons, Hunt, Mather, and Meadows 2009). The group also discussed several longer term goals: mapping the Canadian SoTL landscape in terms of what SoTL programs existed, surveying the STLHE membership regarding their SoTL interests, creating resources and courses on getting started in SoTL, advocating at the national level (including a need for sharing strategies on approaching governments and agencies regarding funding and support), and writing a history of SoTL in Canada to capture the rapidly evolving field. In each case, the advisory board was guided by a focus on how each potential initiative tied to STLHE goals, institutional goals, and disciplinary goals.

At the 2009 conference of ISSoTL, led by Nicola Simmons, and with the strong support of Gary Poole (who was on the ISSoTL board) and Joy Mighty (then president of STLHE), a partnership agreement was signed between STLHE and ISSoTL to acknowledge the organizations' similar missions in furthering the SoTL agenda to improve postsecondary teaching and learning. The intention of this partnership was to develop collaborations between the organizations that might better support moving SoTL forward.

During this time, the advisory panel was acutely aware of a position paper by Poole, Taylor, and Thompson (2007) that drew attention to the questions around what would be needed to advance SoTL in Canada. Several of their recommendations guided the advisory panel's planning, in particular the notion of a national SoTL body and engagement with national advocacy for SoTL. In reviewing its priorities, and with the partnership in place and work underway to establish a strong web presence on the STLHE website to compile resources and track SoTL's history, the SoTL advisory panel decided to refocus its efforts on national advocacy and it was decided to repeat the successful 2005 SoTL Leadership Forum. Consequently,

NEW DIRECTIONS FOR TEACHING AND LEARNING • DOI: 10.1002/tl

in May 2010, a second SoTL Leadership Forum was cohosted in Calgary, Alberta, by STLHE and Mount Royal's Institute for the Scholarship of Teaching and Learning. Over 100 postsecondary institutional leaders attended to consider how SoTL could be further integrated at the institutional level. An article about the event appearing in the national postsecondary magazine *University Affairs* reiterated the call for further action, noting that while much good "on the ground" work was underway, much remained to be done at a national level (Charbonneau 2010).

The notion of national advocacy and grappling with how to best engage in it remained a focus of the SoTL Advisory Panel. In October 2010, members of the panel gave a session at the ISSoTL conference in Liverpool, UK, that explored what we had learned about regional SoTL promotion toward catalyzing the national agenda.

One of our points of celebration was our new national SoTL journal. Earlier in 2010, the tireless efforts of Lynn Taylor and Deb Dawson, with Ken Meadows as managing editor, had seen the launch of STLHE's SoTL journal, *The Canadian Journal for the Scholarship of Teaching and Learning (CJ SoTL)*, to provide an open-access, peer-reviewed, national venue for SoTL scholarship and peer collaboration. As the journal's website outlines, its purpose is to

> advance the scholarship of teaching and learning in Canadian post-secondary institutions. It therefore provides an avenue for a wide range of educators, including faculty members, administrators, academic librarians, educational developers, learning resource specialists, and graduate students, to discuss ways of enhancing student learning experiences through systematic inquiry into teaching and learning in all disciplines. (CJ-SoTL n.d.)

The journal continues to provide a transdisciplinary publication venue for Canadian SoTL work.

In 2011, the STLHE board underwent a restructuring process and the VP positions became chairs. The new STLHE chair of SoTL, Brad Wuetherick, renewed the SoTL advisory panel's membership and the name was changed to the STLHE SoTL Committee. During this time, Brad spearheaded the further development and ultimate publishing of SoTL content for the STLHE website (see www.stlhe.ca/sotl/). Another important venture of this time was to create a national survey of STLHE membership to get a sense of what SoTL programs were in place, and in what ways STLHE could provide support for members' SoTL work. The results of that survey appear in Chapter 2 of this volume.

Development of SoTL Canada

By 2011, STLHE had again reenvisioned its priorities. Part of that discussion included a commitment that as SoTL underpinned all the society's

NEW DIRECTIONS FOR TEACHING AND LEARNING • DOI: 10.1002/tl

activities, it was no longer appropriate to highlight it as a separate pillar. This created a space for the development of a special interest group (SIG) of STLHE, as there were some who wanted to ensure that SoTL continued to be highlighted as part of the national agenda. An invitation was made to the STLHE listserv to invite those interested in forming a SIG to meet at the STLHE annual conference in June. This group discussed areas of interest, which included finding funding sources, leveraging SoTL within academic disciplines, notions of going public, institutional SoTL support, and other resources, all of which, once again, were closely aligned with Poole, Taylor, and Thompson's (2007) call for action. A proposal for a SIG was made by Nicola Simmons (2012) to the STLHE board outlining the goals of the SIG:

> The Scholarship of Teaching and Learning (SoTL) has at its core the goal of improving student learning. This is achieved through scholarly inquiry about learning, about teaching, and about how to best make public the resulting findings. In this way, SoTL shares the goals of STLHE, but at a time when STLHE is moving away from having a dedicated SoTL portfolio, this SIG will provide a targeted opportunity for SoTL scholars to form a community to share findings and challenge, engage in opportunities for broader dissemination of SoTL work, and consider ways to catalyze SoTL initiatives at the institutional, regional, national, and international levels. The name "SoTL Canada" arose organically from the discussions held thus far.

Goals and Subcommittees of the SoTL SIG

1. Engage in a community of practice of SoTL scholars for the purpose of shared resources, research, and problem-solving regarding SoTL issues and questions.
2. Create and contribute to multiple approaches to the dissemination of scholarship about teaching and learning in higher education.
3. Collaborate on effective approaches to building a SoTL culture at institutional, regional, national, and international levels.
4. Serve as a resource and mentoring body for those seeking SoTL information and support.
5. To advocate at all levels, based on the above, for the importance and value of SoTL in enhancing postsecondary student learning. (Simmons, 2012)

The SIG proposal was accepted by the STLHE board, and in 2012, with 35 founding members, SoTL Canada was formed.

By the annual general meeting in June 2012, the earlier ideas had coalesced into a short list of possible ventures. They included SoTL workshops or a preconference session, an institute and writing retreats, peer mentoring, student engagement, the possibility of a standalone SoTL conference in Canada, and a publication to map the Canadian SoTL landscape. By 2013, these, with the exception of the conference, which had been put on hold, became the SIG's working groups (see https://sotlcanada.wordpress.com /sotl-canada-working-groups) and each moved forward on its particular initiatives. For example, a preconference workshop, "Transforming Our Learning Experiences through the Scholarship of Teaching and Learning," was offered at STLHE's annual conference in 2014, and the publication group's work resulted in the volume you are reading now. In addition, to respond to our membership's interest in knowing about SoTL resources and events, and to provide a platform for communicating to them, in 2014, SoTL Canada created its own web presence (see https://sotlcanada.wordpress .com/) that includes a blog to which members contribute.

To support SoTL Canada's ongoing initiatives and to determine from our increasing membership whether the executive directors were still addressing areas of greatest concern to them, in late 2014, we undertook a survey of our members. We obtained ethics approval so that we can make our results public. We not only asked about areas such as interest in workshops and writing retreats but also inquired about the prevalence of student engagement in SoTL across Canadian campuses as well as other campus-specific SoTL initiatives. Analysis of the results is underway; based on our thoughts thus far, we expect to be able to paint a detailed picture of some SoTL initiatives across Canada to provide a comparison across multiple institutions of who is doing what. We see this as a way to contribute to the possibilities for learning from each other and engaging in future collaborations.

Moving Forward

These are some of the steps we have taken thus far. As SoTL Canada moves forward with its leadership role, that move must be focused on gaining ground regarding recognition of SoTL as important scholarly work in Canada. Concurrently, there must be advocacy for funding and other supports at the department and institutional levels, as indicated by a number of chapters in this volume; at the provincial levels, keeping in mind the provincial purview for education; and at the national level, where the larger funding pots are typically to be found.

The role of educational development (ED) centers in promoting SoTL must be further examined. Woodhouse and Force (2010) noted that only slightly over a third of Canadian centers' websites indicated SoTL was central to ED. Questions remain as to the ways in which ED can support and sustain SoTL work and how it can best be integrated into the institutional culture. Chapters in this volume address this issue, but more work is needed.

NEW DIRECTIONS FOR TEACHING AND LEARNING • DOI: 10.1002/tl

Currently, a strong call for action concerns the need to draw students more strongly into the center of SoTL work as coinvestigators, but also in leadership roles. Having a student member of our executive board and highlighting student engagement on our website are two small steps toward this and we continue to seek ways to engage students in SoTL work at the institutional level and beyond.

Other collaborations are equally important. While community colleges have a different workload model and different perspectives on research, increasingly they are the site of a growing tradition of applied research and many are strongly engaged in SoTL at numerous levels. Our college colleagues have much to contribute to SoTL conversations, and it is important that our structures and initiatives invite them as equal partners.

In reflecting on where we have been and where we are going next, we come back to others' ideas. Poole, Taylor, and Thompson (2007) discussed how using SoTL at various levels (institutional, disciplinary, and national) could improve postsecondary educational quality. There continues to be, as they argued, a need for advocacy for SoTL beyond the institutional level. Areas such as support and funding outside the institution require national levels of advocacy, something that takes substantial time and energy. In some ways, we have answered this call: We have a national SoTL organization that is becoming a strong interactive national community, we have had some limited forays into advocacy, we have a national SoTL journal, and we continue to explore additional ways of making work public, including, but not limited to, this volume. Arguably we have made some progress on their recommendations of "advocacy, development, and dissemination" (12); at the same time, it seems we have so far to go.

This leads us to several questions:

- How can we, as a national organization, increase SoTL supports and funding, not only institutionally but also at provincial and national levels?
- How can we, as a national organization, best advocate for SoTL's recognition as valuable scholarship?
- If, in five years, we want to have begun to address these challenges, what steps must be taken now? Who else do we need to invite into the conversation?
- How can we do these things in ways that acknowledge that most of the work is being undertaken as volunteer endeavors? How can we bring committed volunteers together in synergistic networks for greater impact?
- How is it that we have been outlining for 10 years what needs to be done to move SoTL forward in Canada, but we seem to be so slow at doing it? Are we sure we are asking the right questions? Is it simply a question of getting to the "tipping point" (Gladwell 2002)?

SoTL Canada began in 2012 with 35 members, and in 2016, it has a membership over 300. While this is impressive growth, and we can feel pleased at our successes to date, other calls still need to be answered. It is our hope that the chapters in this volume will provide a strong foundation for moving forward with the continued development of SoTL in Canada and may serve as catalysts for this work.

References

Boyer, Ernest. 1990. *Scholarship Reconsidered: Priorities of the Professoriate*. Princeton, NJ: Carnegie Foundation for the Advancement of Teaching.

Charbonneau, Leo. 2010, August 16. "The Scholarship of Teaching and Learning, Five Years On." Available at www.universityaffairs.ca/news/news-article/scholarship-teaching-learning/

Christensen Hughes, Julia, and Joy Mighty, eds. 2010. *Taking Stock: Research on Teaching and Learning*. Montreal, QC and Kingston, ON: McGill-Queen's University Press.

Christensen Hughes, Julia. 2006. "The Scholarship of Teaching and Learning: A Canadian Perspective." Society for Teaching and Learning in Higher Education. Available at www.stlhe.ca/wp-content/uploads/2011/09/SoTLCanadianPerspectiveJan06.pdf

CJ-SoTL. n.d. "The Canadian Journal for the Scholarship of Teaching and Learning." Available at www.cjsotl-rcacea.ca/

Gladwell, Malcolm. 2002. *The Tipping Point: How Little Things Can Make a Big Difference*. Boston, MA: Little, Brown.

Hutchings, Pat, Mary Taylor Huber, and Anthony Ciccone. 2011. *The Scholarship of Teaching and Learning Reconsidered: Institutional Integration and Impact*. San Francisco, CA: Jossey-Bass.

Poole, Gary. 2010, March 28. "Canada: The Scholarship of Teaching and Learning." *University World News*, 117. Available at http://www.universityworldnews.com/article.php?story=20100326112526314

Poole, Gary, and Nicola Simmons. 2013. "The Contributions of the Scholarship of Teaching and Learning to Quality Enhancement in Canada." In *Quality Enhancement in Higher Education: International Perspectives*, edited by George Gordon and Ray Land, 118–128. London: Routledge.

Poole, Gary, K. Lynn Taylor, and John Thompson. 2007. "Using the Scholarship of Teaching and Learning at Disciplinary, National and Institutional Levels to Strategically Improve the Quality of Post-secondary Education." *International Journal for the Scholarship of Teaching and Learning* 1(2): Article 3.

Simmons, Nicola. 2012. "Scholarship of Teaching and Learning in Canada." Available online at www.stlhe.ca/special-interest-groups/scholarship-of-teaching-and-learning-canada/

Simmons, Nicola, Gary Hunt, Jennifer Mather, and Ken Meadows. 2009. *Input to the Draft 2nd Edition of the Tri-Council Policy Statement: Comments and Recommendations Regarding Multi-jurisdictional Research*. Unpublished report submitted to the Canadian Tri-Council for Research.

Society for Teaching and Learning in Higher Education. n.d. "What is SoTL?" Available online at www.stlhe.ca/sotl/what-is-sotl/

Woodhouse, Ros, and Kristin Force. 2010. "Educational Development Websites: What Do They Tell Us about How Canadian Centres Support the Scholarship of Teaching and Learning?" *The Canadian Journal for the Scholarship of Teaching and Learning* 1(1): Article 4.

NICOLA SIMMONS *was the founding chair of SoTL Canada and is currently a member in the faculty of education at Brock University in Ontario.*

GARY POOLE *is the associate director of the School of Population and Public Health and senior scholar in the Centre for Health Education Scholarship at the University of British Columbia.*

NEW DIRECTIONS FOR TEACHING AND LEARNING • DOI: 10.1002/tl

2

This chapter reports on a national study exploring the current state of the Scholarship of Teaching and Learning (SoTL) and assessing the perceptions of Canadian SoTL scholars at the micro (individual), meso (departmental), macro (institutional), and mega (disciplinary) contexts.

The Canadian Teaching Commons: The Scholarship of Teaching and Learning in Canadian Higher Education

Brad Wuetherick, Stan Yu

Over the past two decades, the Scholarship of Teaching and Learning (SoTL) has grown into an international movement of individuals and organizations dedicated to improving student learning in higher education (Kwo 2007), and Canadian teachers, researchers, and educational developers have played a significant role in advancing the movement (Schönwetter and Bateman 2010). Within Canada, however, the climate for teaching and learning in higher education and SoTL has been the subject of an ongoing conversation. There have been several studies exploring the state of SoTL across the country, particularly looking at the SoTL community at the level of individual institutions (Poole and Simmons 2013; Poole, Taylor, and Thompson 2007). They point to several exemplars of "well-supported" institutions across the country that have had success in raising the quality, quantity, and profile of SoTL work, whether through successful institutional granting and mentoring programs or university-wide cross-disciplinary research centers. There are, however, just as many examples of SoTL being championed within environments where the efforts would not be considered central to the institution.

This chapter explores the current state of SoTL in Canada in what might be termed the Canadian "teaching commons" (Huber and Hutchings 2005). It attempts to unpack the perceptions of Canadian SoTL scholars at the individual, departmental, institutional, and disciplinary levels. By doing so, we hope that the SoTL community in Canada and around the world can continue to engage in meaningful conversations about how to advance

New Directions for Teaching and Learning, no. 146, Summer 2016 © 2016 Wiley Periodicals, Inc.
Published online in Wiley Online Library (wileyonlinelibrary.com) • DOI: 10.1002/tl.20183

SoTL as a critical aspect of the teaching and research landscape in higher education.

The Teaching Commons

Huber and Hutchings (2005) posited the emergence of a global *teaching commons*, a conceptual space in which communities of educators committed to inquiry and innovation come together across institutional, disciplinary, and national boundaries to share, debate, critique, and build on ideas about teaching and learning and use them to meet the challenges of educating students. The idea of the teaching commons is a manifestation of the growing community of teaching and learning that has arisen as teaching has moved from "private to community property" (Shulman 1993, 6). Huber and Hutchings (2005, 5) argue that "without a functioning commons it is hard for pedagogical knowledge to circulate, deepen through debate and critique, and inform the kinds of innovation so important to higher education today."

The Current Study

An anonymous electronic survey, adapted from the 2004 Carnegie Academy for Scholarship of Teaching and Learning (CASTL) survey (Huber and Hutchings 2005), was administered to the Society for Teaching and Learning in Higher Education (STLHE) membership in the summer of 2012 as part of a pilot study. A total of 140 responses were obtained with representation spanning all provinces. There was a relatively balanced range of respondents across academic ranks, types of institutions, genders, and ages (see Table 2.1). Conversely, the respondents were not a representative sample by discipline (see Table 2.1). All results presented throughout this paper are reported as a percentage based on respondents' levels of agreement from a six-item Likert scale, ranging from strongly disagree (1) to strongly agree (6).

Understanding the Canadian Teaching Commons

Although the original Carnegie study does not use this framework, the survey matches the model of exploring SoTL work at the micro level (the level of individual SoTL capacity), meso level (the level of department and faculty), macro level (the level of institution), and mega level (the level of disciplines and interdisciplinary connections, as well as the level of national and international connections) (Poole 2009; Poole and Simmons 2013; Simmons 2011; Williams et al. 2013).

Micro Level. The survey explored a number of dimensions at the micro level of the individual SoTL practitioner, including the range and intensity of their participation in SoTL and the impact of their participation on

Table 2.1. Demographics of STLHE SoTL Survey Respondents

Academic Rank	n	Type of Institution	n	Gender	n	Age	n	Disciplinary Affiliation	n
Full Professor	33	Medical/Doctoral	44	Female	59	Under 40	24	Health Sciences	9
Associate Professor	19	Comprehensive	40	Male	42	41–50	31	Natural Sciences	30
Assistant Professor	15	Primarily Undergraduate	18			51–60	38	Social Sciences and Humanities	74
Instructor/Lecturer	8	College or Technical Institute	20			61+	20		
Administrative Staff	5	Other	4						
Other	5								

the perceptions and practices of their own teaching and career advancement. In our sample, approximately three-quarters of respondents replied that they have presented at a conference dedicated to teaching and learning, and more than half (57 percent) of respondents have presented their SoTL project(s) at discipline-based conferences. An equivalent number (57 percent) have published their SoTL projects in journals or books, and 70 percent responded that they were actively working on a SoTL project at the time when they completed the questionnaire. Ninety-four percent of respondents have collaborated with colleagues at their institutions in framing and investigating questions about teaching and learning, and 92 percent have participated in SoTL professional development at their institutions. Slightly more than three-quarters of respondents (77 percent) further reported that the supportive attitudes of departmental colleagues were present in their context, the majority of whom indicated this was important to their work (60 percent).

When asked about funding for projects on teaching and learning, it was found that three-quarters (76 percent) of respondents reported that campus funding was present, though only slightly more than half (53 percent) felt it was important to their SoTL work. On the other hand, 49 percent of respondents reported that funding from external sources was not present, and only 29 percent stated that external funding was present and important to their work. Along with sources of support, this study gauged respondents' opinions about the extent to which certain constraints continue to hinder their engagement in SoTL. Respondents identified that the tension between demands for research productivity and SoTL remains the primary obstacle (91 percent), and continued confusion among faculty colleagues as to what constitutes SoTL (91 percent) was a major concern.

As a result of their involvement in SoTL, respondents reported a significant impact on their perceptions of, and practices within, their own teaching and their students' learning. Respondents were most likely to agree that becoming involved in SoTL has contributed to their excitement about teaching (93 percent) and changed their expectations for both their teaching (94 percent) and their students' learning (93 percent). In terms of their individual teaching practices, the respondents were very likely to report that their involvement in SoTL has contributed to them changing the designs of their courses (99 percent) and the kinds of assessments they used in their courses (94 percent). Overall, the majority of respondents felt that the quality of their students' learning has changed since their involvement in SoTL (94 percent).

We further asked respondents about the role played by their involvement in SoTL in their career advancement. Slightly more than half (52 percent) of respondents cited that tenure and promotion policies that encourage SoTL do exist and are important to their work, although 39 percent of respondents found that these policies were not present. Of the respondents who had applicable personal experiences, many reported that their involvement in SoTL strengthened their most recent merit review (45 percent), hiring decision (48 percent), tenure application (53 percent), and promotion to full professor (57 percent), while very few respondents (4 percent or less in each category) reported that their SoTL involvement had weakened their case for career advancement. A sizeable group of respondents, however, were uncertain of the role that their involvement in SoTL played in the decision making for merit (55 percent), hiring (35 percent), tenure (34 percent), and promotion to full professor (39 percent). In addition, more than two-thirds of respondents reported that their participation in SoTL has created a major new career focus (68 percent) or new opportunities at their institution (72 percent). The responses were bifurcated about whether respondents had been recruited for a new position because of SoTL (52 percent in agreement). A slight majority of respondents (54 percent) also agreed that a fear of making teaching public could undermine faculty members' academic freedom and hence impact their involvement in SoTL.

Meso Level.   At the meso level of the institution (in particular the culture of departments on campuses), the results were mixed. On the one hand, our findings show that there is some evidence of departmental support for SoTL at institutions across Canada, particularly in terms of taking SoTL into consideration in hiring practices (65 percent) and receiving encouragement from department chairs to be involved in SoTL (64 percent). On the other hand, we found that respondents were uncertain about whether their department has broadened the criteria for assessing faculty teaching performance to reflect SoTL over the past five years (56 percent). The same was true about assessing faculty research performance (47 percent). While respondents were inclined to agree that other faculty members within their departments are actively working on SoTL (66 percent), there were a surprising number of respondents who reported that their departmental colleagues find their work on SoTL to be problematic (54 percent). When asked whether departmental norms encourage participation in SoTL, we found it almost evenly split in terms of agreement and disagreement (50 percent). Overall, the survey illustrates that more work is needed in terms of departmental culture.

Macro Level.   At the macro, or institutional, level, it was found that people in formal or academic leadership roles at their institutions have taken steps toward supporting SoTL (70 percent). With regard to the perceptions of whether institutional policies integrate SoTL, respondents agreed that there have been some efforts to broaden the criteria for assessing teaching performance to reflect SoTL (63 percent), whereas there was less agreement about whether efforts have been made to broaden the criteria for assessing research performance to reflect SoTL (56 percent). A very similar response was found amongst respondents when asked whether SoTL is integrated into other institutional priorities and initiatives (60 percent). This level of agreement was found to be even lower when asked if SoTL at the respondents' institutions was widespread (50 percent). Respondents were

NEW DIRECTIONS FOR TEACHING AND LEARNING • DOI: 10.1002/tl

most likely to disagree that their institution provides adequate campus-level funding opportunities for engaging in SoTL (35 percent) and incorporates criteria for promotion that reflect the principles of SoTL (44 percent). One of the only questions respondents were slightly more positive about at the macro level is that the criteria for institutional teaching awards are consistent with the principles of SoTL (72 percent). Finally, the majority of respondents generally agreed that the lack of leadership among top-level administrators remained an obstacle to their involvement in SoTL (78 percent).

Mega Level.   The survey also assessed respondents' opinions of the mega level, as represented in the disciplinary and interdisciplinary context. In particular, the survey explored changes in the quantity and quality of venues for publication and dissemination in the field of SoTL. In terms of the number of journals devoted to teaching within their field of study, the results were divided evenly amongst respondents who felt there were no changes in quantity versus respondents who felt there has been an increase in quantity. Almost two-thirds of respondents (65 percent) further felt that there has been a higher standard of quality in the number of journals on teaching and learning within their fields of study over the past five years. In terms of the number of SoTL articles in the top journals of their fields, a majority of respondents reported both an increase in quantity (53 percent) and an increase in quality (68 percent). Similar findings were identified with regard to the number and quality of sessions about SoTL at the annual conferences in the respondents' disciplines. Professional development activities related to SoTL and the efforts of professional associations to encourage SoTL were present for the vast majority of respondents (89 percent) and were important to their work (82 percent).

Conclusion: Advancing the Teaching Commons in Canada

This study confirms that the current state of SoTL in Canada is varied and highly influenced by the context of individual SoTL practitioners. There was (at times limited) agreement amongst respondents about progress toward departmental and institutional culture changes around SoTL. Overall, respondents demonstrated a belief that SoTL is contributing positively to careers (though there is still some uncertainty), that there are increases in quantity and quality of SoTL research output and dissemination, and that there are some positive changes happening with respect to disciplinary, institutional, and departmental support for SoTL. There were, however, high levels of agreement about tensions and constraints placed on faculty interested in SoTL and the challenges faced in changing departmental (and institutional) cultures to support SoTL, as well as a general perception of a lack of administrative leadership in championing SoTL moving forward on their respective campuses.

It has been identified that organizational culture within higher education is complex and potentially intimidating, particularly when trying to change that culture, "yet the success of institutional transformation largely depends on the ability of change agents to understand culture" (Craig 2004, 54). Shining a light on the organizational SoTL culture across Canada, as well as the areas of progress and continuing barriers, as attempted in this study, is meant to encourage both institutional academic leaders and SoTL scholars in Canada (and elsewhere) to continue to work toward advancing the teaching commons on their respective campuses and in their respective disciplines. Whether by continuing to provide evidence about and championing innovations in teaching practices at the micro to mega levels, or aligning individual (micro) SoTL projects with institutional (macro) assessment projects, there are a number of key strategies that have been identified in the literature to further enhance institutional SoTL integration and impact (Hutchings, Huber, and Ciccone 2011).

Williams and colleagues (2013) argue that to continue to develop the teaching commons, higher education institutions and disciplines need to focus on improving communication and dissemination, further developing social networks between SoTL scholars, and continuing to provide sustained support for SoTL at the micro through macro (and mega) levels. In particular, they call on individuals at the macro level (for example, institutional academic leaders) to serve as agents of culture change, as catalysts for the development of social networks, and as champions of enhanced and sustained support for SoTL (Martensson et al. 2011; Williams et al. 2013).

While the size, diversity, and momentum of the teaching commons are growing, "the movement to do so is, we believe, one of the most hopeful signs that the academy will be able to fulfill its changing teaching mission in the years to come" (Huber and Hutchings 2005, 14). The continued effort to advance SoTL, from the micro to the mega levels, will ensure that the "passionate energy vibrating in the SoTL commons" will continue to inspire our enhanced understandings of teaching and learning at the institutional, disciplinary, and international levels (Kwo 2007, 3). Indeed, in such a teaching commons, whether in Canada or around the world, we can collectively ensure that SoTL not only helps us do things better but also that we do better things for and with our students (Elton 2000).

References

Craig, Clarissa M. 2004. "Higher Education Culture and Organizational Change in the 21st Century." *The Community College Enterprise: A Journal of Research & Practice* 10(1): 79–87.

Elton, Lewis. 2000, January 7–9. "Dangers of Doing the Wrong Thing Righter." Paper presented at *Evaluate and Improve – Conference of the Humanities and Arts Higher Education Network*, Milton Keynes, UK.

Huber, Mary and Pat Hutchings. 2005. *The Advancement of Learning: Building the Teaching Commons*. San Francisco, CA: Jossey-Bass.

Hutchings, Pat, Mary Huber, and Tony Ciccone. 2011. *Scholarship of Teaching and Learning Reconsidered: Institutional Integration and Impact*. San Francisco, CA: Jossey-Bass.

Kwo, Ora. 2007. "SoTL in the Commons: Elephant, Authenticity and Journey." *International Journal of the Scholarship of Teaching and Learning* 1(2): Article 4.

Martensson, Katarina, Torgny Roxa, and Thomas Olsson. 2011. "Developing a Quality Culture through the Scholarship of Teaching and Learning." *Higher Education Research and Development* 30(1): 51–62.

Poole, Gary. 2009, May 25–27. "The Pursuit of the Scholarship of Teaching and Learning in Canada: Good, but Not Good Enough." Keynote presentation at the Annual Canadian Society for Studies in Higher Education Conference, Ottawa, ON.

Poole, Gary, K. Lynn Taylor, and John Thompson. 2007. "Using the Scholarship of Teaching and Learning at Disciplinary, National and Institutional Levels to Strategically Improve the Quality of Post-secondary Education." *International Journal of the Scholarship of Teaching and Learning* 1(2): Article 3.

Poole, Gary, and Nicola Simmons. 2013. "Contributions of the Scholarship of Teaching and Learning to Quality Enhancement in Canada." In *Enhancing Quality in Higher Education: International Perspectives*, edited by Ray Land and George Gordon. London: Routledge.

Schönwetter, Dieter, and Diane Bateman. 2010. "An Introduction by the Editors." *Canadian Journal for the Scholarship of Teaching and Learning*, 1(1): Article 1.

Shulman, Lee. 1993. "Teaching as Community Property: Putting an End to Pedagogical Solitude." *Change* 25(6): 6–7.

Simmons, Nicola. 2011, June 15–18. "From There to Here and Here to There: Is SoTL Impact Everywhere?" Presentation at the Society for Teaching and Learning in Higher Education Annual Conference, Saskatoon, SK.

Williams, Andrea, Roselynn Verwood, Theresa A. Beery, Helen Dalton, James McKinnon, Karen Strickland, Jessica Pace, and Gary Poole. 2013. "The Power of Social Networks: A Model for Weaving the Scholarship of Teaching and Learning into Institutional Culture." *Teaching and Learning Inquiry* 1(2): 49–62.

BRAD WUETHERICK *is the executive director of learning and teaching in the Office of the Provost and vice president academic and Centre for Learning and Teaching at Dalhousie University.*

STAN YU *is a research associate with the International Centre for Northern Governance and Development and former research and program evaluation analyst with the Gwenna Moss Centre for Teaching Effectiveness at the University of Saskatchewan.*

NEW DIRECTIONS FOR TEACHING AND LEARNING • DOI: 10.1002/tl

3

This chapter describes a SoTL program at Simon Fraser University that focuses on the importance of analyzing the internal coherence and alignment of the program design and the thinking underpinning the design as the first steps in evaluating effectiveness or impact.

The Intentional Design of a SoTL Initiative

Cheryl Amundsen, Esma Emmioglu, Veronica Hotton, Gregory Hum, Cindy Xin

Stes, Min-Leliveld, Gijbels, and Van Petegem (2010) argue that without detailed published descriptions of the design of educational development programs and processes, we cannot hope to understand what features of educational development make it effective. Amundsen and Wilson (2012) agree and suggest that the first step to evaluating effectiveness is to analyze the program design, attending to evidence of alignment and coherence in the underlying rationale, the learning goals, and the strategies used to assess effectiveness or impact. Reviews of the educational development literature (Steinert, Mann, Centeno, Dolmans, Spencer, Gelula, and Prideaux 2006; Stes, Min-Leliveld, Gijbels, and Van Petegem 2010) have, in our view, typically taken a narrow view of evaluation or impact (Kreber and Brook 2001). That is, too great a focus is placed on outcomes in terms of individual surface features of programs (for example, assessing all "workshops" similarly) without adequate consideration of what outcomes are reasonable given the particular details of the program design.

Consistent with this perspective, the focus of this paper is the analysis of the design of a Scholarship of Teaching and Learning (SoTL) initiative with attention to the internal coherence and alignment of program elements and the literature that informed the thinking underpinning the design. We begin by describing the direct link from program goals to activities faculty engage in to strategies designed to assess effectiveness or impact. This is followed by a discussion of the literature that most informed the design and with which it is most aligned. As noted, we consider this type of intentional design and analysis as a first step in determining the effectiveness of a program and, just as importantly, in allowing us to understand what design features support desired outcomes.

NEW DIRECTIONS FOR TEACHING AND LEARNING, no. 146, Summer 2016 © 2016 Wiley Periodicals, Inc.
Published online in Wiley Online Library (wileyonlinelibrary.com) • DOI: 10.1002/tl.20184

Our SoTL program, Teaching and Learning Development Grants Program, is intended as a broad educational development strategy aimed at enhancing teaching and learning and encouraging conversations and collaborations about teaching across the institution (www.sfu.ca/tlgrants). It is funded directly by the vice president (academic), and is facilitated by the Institute for the Study of Teaching and Learning in the Disciplines in partnership with the Teaching and Learning Centre. Since late 2011, the program has provided over 160 small grants of up to $5,000 to faculty to systematically investigate questions about teaching and learning of interest to them. We seek to achieve two broad goals through this program:

1. Support faculty members to enhance their knowledge and practice as related to teaching and learning (Clarke and Hollingsworth 2002)
2. Engage faculty in teaching as a socially situated practice (Billett 2009, 2010).

Figure 3.1 shows the basic design of our program linked to the two goals stated previously. The following discussion of the program design is organized by the four broad program elements: project development,

Figure 3.1. Program Design

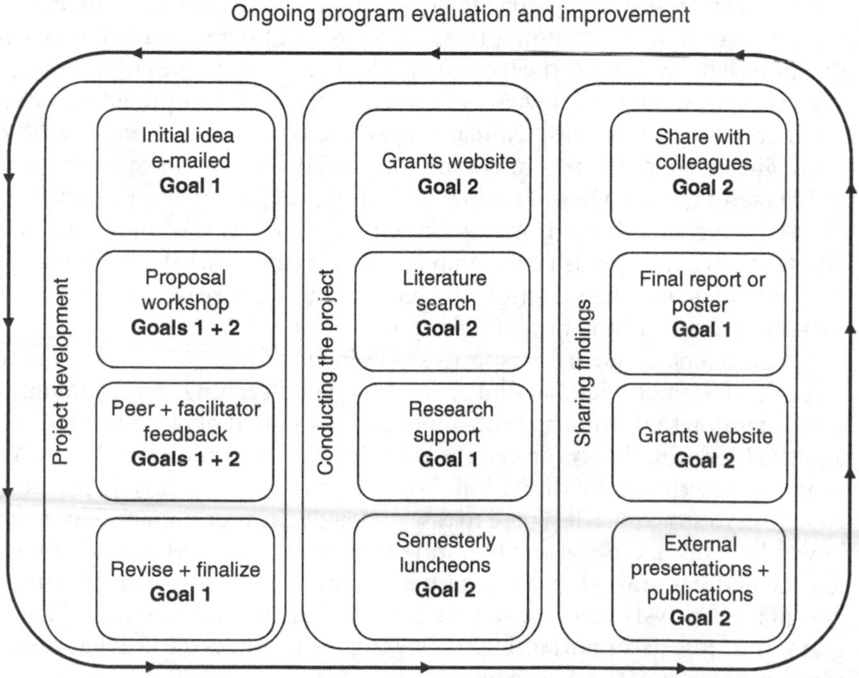

Ongoing program evaluation and improvement

conducting the project, sharing findings, and ongoing improvement of the design.

Project Development

Two 2-hour proposal development workshop sessions are required and are offered two to three times per semester. The primary applicant attends, but other faculty or graduate students who will be involved in conducting the project may also attend, and many do. Faculty arrive at the first proposal development workshop session having submitted their initial project idea(s) via e-mail. The focus of the first session is to clarify the questions and/or purposes of the project that will provide the structure of the investigation. In between the first and second sessions, initial proposal drafts are submitted to all who attended the first session. The intention is to foster a collaborative process, wherein each applicant develops his or her own project proposal but also provides feedback (oral and written) to others. The discussions in the workshops are generally lively, and faculty become quite engaged in one another's project ideas. After the second session, one-to-one feedback continues between the applicant and the workshop facilitators until the proposal is finalized. Our program design differs from most grant programs in that grants are not awarded on a competitive basis; if a faculty member follows the process to finalization of the proposal, he or she will receive funding (*note:* we have not yet exceeded available funding). This decision is based on our view of the grants program as an educational development strategy, and from that point of view, we want to support all faculty who want to investigate teaching and learning and are willing to develop quality proposals.

All projects must directly link to enhancing student learning. The majority of projects have focused on a course (or courses) with the introduction and evaluation of a new teaching approach or method (for example, team-based learning, group exams). Several projects are design-oriented projects in which instructional tools are built and piloted (for example, a website to teach historical thinking). A few projects design and evaluate a program to support an entire academic program (such as workshops integrated into first-year courses to address high drop-out rates). Finally, a few projects work at the level of the program curriculum (for example, building an online tool to track curriculum changes). A detailed budget is part of the proposal and must directly link expenses to project goals. The majority of the funding across projects is used to hire undergraduate or graduate student research assistants (RAs) who carry out a variety of tasks with the faculty investigator(s) (for example, development of course materials, collecting, and analyzing data). Other expenses have included software and hiring individuals with specific skills (such as a videographer, web developer). Descriptions of all projects that have been funded and other

NEW DIRECTIONS FOR TEACHING AND LEARNING • DOI: 10.1002/tl

information (for example, eligible expenses, project proposal guidelines) about the grants program can be found at www.sfu.ca/tlgrants.

Conducting the Project

We continue to support faculty during the conduct of their projects. Soon after the grant proposal is finalized, a member of our team will read the finalized proposal, develop a brief summary, and ask the faculty member to edit it before it is uploaded to our website. The website has been a valuable resource in many ways, such as that it provides a venue for faculty contemplating a grant to see what others have done and a way for faculty working on similar ideas to connect. We do not ask faculty to include a literature review as part of the proposal because few are conversant with the relevant literature. Instead, team members offer, once the proposal is finalized, to identify a few examples of educational research relevant to each project, and in this way, faculty are connected with the work of the wider scholarly community, which they may investigate further. Since many of the projects involve gathering feedback from students using surveys or questionnaires, we have developed an instructional process for faculty and student RAs comprised initial instruction and ongoing support through consultations. Attendees learn how to create instruments and analyze the resulting data. We also offer "just in time" support as needed. We are growing this aspect of our support, as we identify other needed knowledge and skills (for example, analysis of qualitative data). Finally, we organize luncheon meetings two to three times each year to bring together faculty who are conducting projects to share their progress and their challenges in conducting their grant projects.

Sharing Findings

Faculty are required to share their project findings with departmental or other close faculty colleagues; this may be as informal as inviting a few interested colleagues for coffee. Verwoord and Poole's chapter in this volume also discusses the power of informal conversations. Many faculty have also organized more formal presentations within their departments. In our experience, it is this local dissemination that has been most effective in spreading project ideas and findings and in encouraging other faculty to adapt and implement their colleagues' project ideas in their own teaching. Faculty submit final reports or posters in which they return to the questions in their grant proposals to organize and report findings. Faculty may also present the findings in the form of a poster at the annual Symposium on Teaching and Learning sponsored by the Teaching and Learning Centre.

Final reports and posters are uploaded to the grants website along with project descriptions; this way, we have a complete "public" record of each grant. Many faculty have also presented their project findings at disciplinary conferences, and some have published their project findings.

Ongoing Improvement of the Design

Ongoing improvement of the program is an integral part of our program design. We are interested in the learning of individual faculty members who conduct the projects (our first goal), but we are also interested in the connections and collaborations that are made during the conduct of the project and after (our second goal). For this reason, we have identified assessment points at three levels of the institution: individual, departmental, and institutional (Norton 2008). We are actively working with three sources of data: surveys for faculty and student RAs, faculty interviews, and project documents (for example, proposals and final reports). The anonymous survey addresses our two program goals, probing instructors' perceptions of the grants program across the three levels of evaluation, focusing on their learning, experiences, and actions taken. It is organized into five sections. Sections one and two (individual/course level, general implications) center primarily on our first program goal and the individual level of evaluation; sections three and four (project teams, dissemination of findings) seek primarily to assess our second goal and the departmental and institutional levels of evaluation; and sections five and six (overall evaluation, open-ended questions) seek to gather formative information helpful to the ongoing improvement of the program design. Short "coffee break" interviews seek more detail about anonymous survey responses. We are taking several directions with the content analysis, including identifying research designs used and ways in which student learning is assessed. We describe our evaluation framework in detail, provide copies of instruments used, and report our preliminary findings in another paper (Hum, Amundsen, and Emmioglu 2015).

Alignment of the Design with the Literature

In addition to analyzing the internal coherence and alignment of our SoTL program design as described previously, we also have intentionally aligned it with literature addressing the growth of professional knowledge and institutional change. Most influential to our thinking in support of our first goal (to enhance individual knowledge and practice as related to teaching and learning) was the interconnected model of teacher professional growth developed by Clarke and Hollingsworth (2002). While this model was developed to explain the process by which K–12 teachers gain professional knowledge and enhance their practice, we found it especially useful in our context in helping us to think about how a grant project could result in learning beyond the specific focus of the project itself, perhaps generalizing to other aspects of a faculty member's teaching practice. Thus, we designed the grants to be small research projects representing "professional experimentation," a notion central to Clarke and Hollingsworth's model (2002, 950).

Trigwell and Shale (2004) argue that descriptions and definitions of SoTL have not paid enough attention to students but rather have focused almost exclusively on the development of individual instructor knowledge and practice. They advocate for "deliberate, collaborative meaning-making with students" (531) and coin the term "pedagogic resonance" (524) to reflect the direct link between teacher knowledge and student learning. In the design of our grants program, we have focused on student learning in two ways. First, as noted previously, by far the majority of the grants projects investigate the effectiveness of a new (to the instructor) approach or method, and in each of these projects, data are collected about student achievement and/or students' perceptions of their learning. For many faculty, this creates a new or enhanced dynamic around teaching, because the focus moves away from simply what they are doing as teachers to a focus on how what they do and what students do support learning. A second way in which our design involves students is as RAs for specific projects. In this role, undergraduate and graduate students are part of a team investigating teaching and learning and experience firsthand research about teaching and learning.

In addressing our second goal, to engage faculty in teaching as a socially situated practice, we drew inspiration from Billett's (2009, 2010) theory of coparticipation, which comes from a literature generally referred to as "workplace learning." While both Clarke and Hollingsworth (2002) and Trigwell and Shale (2004) focus on the development of the individual, Billett argues that this perspective does not acknowledge the importance of social and contextual elements of practice. In the context and structure of higher education, teaching can be quite an isolated activity, a situation that must be disrupted if institutional change with respect to teaching and learning is desired. Workload structures often do not encourage team-teaching, and many faculty report that they rarely discuss teaching with their colleagues. In the design of our grants program, we have addressed this right from the onset in the proposal development workshops where faculty shape their project ideas with colleagues in attendance and with workshop facilitators. We encourage individuals to talk with others in different academic units with similar grant projects, and our growing database of projects makes this increasingly natural. The grants website also provides an opportunity to learn about the project work of others across the university and within one's own department/faculty. Luncheons each semester bring grant recipients together to share project findings and challenges, and these events have facilitated some additional project collaborations. Essentially, the basis of our second goal is to encourage faculty to start thinking about teaching as a socially situated activity and to provide opportunities for them to experience it.

Dissemination of findings has been understood as a primary characteristic of SoTL since the notion was first proposed by Boyer (1990). The emphasis has been, however, on formal dissemination in the form of conference presentations and, especially, publications. Since we conceive of the grants program as an educational development strategy, our primary focus is the enhancement of teaching and learning at our own institution. Therefore, while we certainly value the fact that many of the grants projects are of high enough quality to be presented elsewhere or to be published, we are more interested in project findings being shared with interested departmental colleagues, as we think this is where teaching practice can most directly be influenced. In this regard, we are aligned with Theall and Centra (2001) and Kreber (2013), who argue for more informal dissemination and opportunities for collegial interaction throughout the SoTL process:

> Equally important, collaborative efforts bring the life of the classroom into the day-to-day reach and attention of units and individuals across campus and reinforce the notion that, rather than being in a closed society apart from the academic community, they are partners with the rest of the institutional community in achieving excellence. (Theall and Centra 2001, 36)

The multilevel evaluation framework (individual, departmental, and institutional) we use to guide ongoing improvement in the program design was adapted from other SoTL researchers (for example, Norton 2008). To best capture these levels, we use and consider multiple sources and types of data and triangulate between them. Ultimately, we want to understand not only what to track and document at each level but also the interaction between the levels. In this respect, we draw on Maki's (2010) notion of building an institutional process of inquiry over time and across multiple levels of the university, using a "cycle of inquiry" that deepens as we come to better understand the scope of what we are assessing. This provides the opportunity for depth and emergent findings.

Conclusion

We argue that examining the internal coherence and alignment of a program design and the thinking underpinning it constitutes a first step in evaluating effectiveness. Sound and intentional design is, we believe, foundational in determining effectiveness or impact. Our intentional design positions SoTL as more than a way to enhance individual faculty knowledge and practice related to teaching; it also seeks to support cross-faculty conversations and collaborations that we think are a step in the direction of institutional change. Detailed and reasoned descriptions of SoTL practice such as we have provided are necessary if we are to build upon previous practice and ultimately understand how best to design such programs and what makes them effective.

NEW DIRECTIONS FOR TEACHING AND LEARNING • DOI: 10.1002/tl

References

Amundsen, Cheryl, and Mary Wilson. 2012. "Are We Asking the Right Questions? A Conceptual Review of Educational Development in Higher Education." *Review of Educational Research* 82(1): 90–126.

Billett, Stephen. 2009. "Personal Epistemologies, Work and Learning." *Educational Research Review* 4(3): 210–219.

Billett, Stephen. 2010. "Lifelong Learning and Self: Work, Subjectivity and Learning." *Studies in Continuing Education* 32(1): 1–16.

Boyer, Ernest. 1990. *Scholarship Reconsidered: Priorities of the Professoriate.* Princeton, NJ: The Carnegie Foundation for the Advancement of Teaching.

Clarke, David, and Hilary Hollingsworth. 2002. "Elaborating a Model of Teacher Professional Growth." *Teaching and Teacher Education* 18: 947–967.

Hum, Gregory, Cheryl Amundsen, and Esma Emmioglu. 2015. "A Framework for Evaluating the Scholarship of Teaching and Learning: Our Process, Challenges, Findings and Insights." *Studies in Educational Evaluation* 46: 29–38.

Kreber, Carolin. 2013. *Authenticity in and Through Teaching in Higher Education: The Transformative Potential of the Scholarship of Teaching.* London: Routledge.

Kreber, Carolin, and Paula Brook. 2001. "Impact Evaluation of Educational Development Programs." *International Journal for Academic Development* 6: 96–108.

Maki, Peggy. 2010. *Assessing for Learning,* 2nd ed. Sterling, VA: Stylus.

Norton, Lin S. 2008. *Action Research in Teaching and Learning: A Practical Guide to Conducting Pedagogical Research in Universities.* Abingdon, UK: Routledge.

Steinert, Yvonne, Karen Mann, Angel Centeno, Diana Dolmans, John Spencer, Mark Gelula, and David Prideaux. 2006. "A Systematic Review of Faculty Development Initiatives Designed to Improve Teaching Effectiveness in Medical Education." *Medical Teacher* 28: 497–526.

Stes, Ann, Mariska Min-Leliveld, David Gijbels, and Peter Van Petegem. 2010. "The Impact of Instructional Development in Higher Education: The State-of-the-Art of the Research." *Educational Research Review* 5: 25–49.

Theall, Michael, and John A. Centra. 2001. "Assessing the Scholarship of Teaching: Valid Decisions from Valid Evidence." *New Directions for Teaching and Learning* 86: 31–44.

Trigwell, Keith, and Suzanne Shale. 2004. "Student Learning and the Scholarship of University Teaching." *Studies in Higher Education* 29(4): 523–536.

CHERYL AMUNDSEN *is a professor in the faculty of education and director of the Institute for the Study of Teaching and Learning in the Disciplines at Simon Fraser University.*

ESMA EMMIOGLU *is an assistant professor at Gaziosmanpaşa University, Turkey.*

VERONICA HOTTON *graduated from Simon Fraser University and is an instructor at Portland State University.*

GREGORY HUM *is a doctoral candidate in the faculty of education at Simon Fraser University.*

CINDY XIN *is an educational consultant in the Teaching and Learning Centre at Simon Fraser University.*

4

This chapter presents the case study of Renaissance College at the University of New Brunswick, discussing the faculty's achievements, challenges, and outlook for the future in the context of the scholarship of teaching and learning in Canada.

The Scholarship of Teaching and Learning (SoTL) at Renaissance College (University of New Brunswick): A Case Study of SoTL at the Faculty Level

Thomas Mengel

Renaissance College (RC) is the University of New Brunswick's (UNB) faculty for interdisciplinary leadership education. RC's mandate includes experimenting with innovative pedagogy and contributing to the Scholarship of Teaching and Learning (SoTL), which at RC has been defined as "faculty research about their teaching" (Zundel and Mengel 2007, 70), at the larger university and beyond. While some progress was made over the past 15 years, this mandate is far from being successfully completed.

In 2001, RC, originally staffed by faculty members seconded from other UNB faculties, accepted its initial cohort. RC's mission was and still is "to provide high quality education for UNB students, educate leaders for the new millennium, and create an exemplary model of post-secondary education" (Zundel, Bishop, Carr, Clarke, Colford, Mengel et al. 2006, 5). In its flagship program, students graduate with a bachelor of philosophy in interdisciplinary leadership studies after being exposed to a multitude of perspectives in interdisciplinary courses, national and international internships, and a minor taken outside of RC in a traditional discipline.

In this chapter, I will first review RC's engagement with SoTL at the individual and at the college levels and in the context of UNB as a whole. Second, I will describe the development of RC's contributions in the light of the initial growth period (2001–2007), under challenging budgetary constraints (2008–2011), and in the context of encouraging initial steps of potential consolidation (since 2012). Finally, I will summarize the key

NEW DIRECTIONS FOR TEACHING AND LEARNING, no. 146, Summer 2016 © 2016 Wiley Periodicals, Inc.
Published online in Wiley Online Library (wileyonlinelibrary.com) • DOI: 10.1002/tl.20185

observations of RC's contribution to SoTL and conclude with some lessons learned both for RC and for other colleges and universities interested in SoTL.

RC's Engagement with SoTL

This section will review the various levels of engagement of individuals and the college in SoTL.

Presentations and Publications of RC Teaching Faculty.   Early in the process, RC teaching faculty (called *integrators* to highlight their role in integrating the various learning experiences and activities)—particularly the two full-time tenure track faculty members and the dean—engaged in SoTL by presenting the results of their studies at various teaching and learning conferences; some of these presentations were published in peer-reviewed conference proceedings or journal articles (Kuruganti and Zundel 2004; Mengel 2014, 2010a, 2010c, 2008, 2006a, 2006b; Mengel et al. 2006; Valk and Mengel 2007; Zundel and Mengel 2007; Zundel et al. 2006). A review of programs for conferences on teaching and learning in Atlantic Canada between 2000 and 2014 revealed that 13 RC integrators had contributed 26 presentations; although the topics presented cover a wider range of SoTL perspectives, their foci was on assessment of student learning (six presentations), student motivation (five presentations), and learning outcomes (four presentations).

Similarly, particularly the two full-time tenure-track RC integrators have presented and published their SoTL projects at conferences specific to the fields of leadership and project management (for example, Mengel 2010c; Mengel et al. 2006; Valk and Mengel 2007). Furthermore, some of the core SoTL-related interests of integrators are also reflected in peer-reviewed publications on project management education, leadership development and education, outcome-based education, and curricular evolution and assessment (Couturier and Mengel 2008; Mengel 2010b, 2008; Thomas and Mengel 2014; Zundel and Mengel 2007). A key component supporting the involvement of full-time and tenure-track faculty members in SoTL may also be the fact that presentations and publications in this field have been recognized by the respective tenure and promotion committees at UNB at a level comparable to the more "traditional" discipline- or field-specific scholarly work of faculty; two full-time faculty members at RC have received tenure and were promoted to professor also based on their engagement in SoTL.

Finally, RC deans and faculty members are recognized for their teaching prior to or during their tenure at RC; this further demonstrates the commitment of RC and its leadership to teaching and to SoTL. Dr. Pierre Zundel, a founding member of RC and dean of RC from 2004 to 2009, was awarded the 3M National Teaching Fellowship by the Society for Teaching and Learning in Higher Education (STLHE) in 2003; Dr. Ted Needham, who contributed to the RC program in various roles prior to being the dean of RC from 2009 to 2013, was awarded the UNB University Teaching Professorship in 2003; and finally, instructors and administrative staff at RC have jointly engaged in a project resulting in the Alan Blizzard Award by the STLHE in 2006.

RC's Alan Blizzard Award.   This STLHE award, bestowed in recognition of collaborative projects that evidentially improve student learning, demonstrates the successful commitment of the whole college to SoTL at the time. The goal of the project leading to the Alan Blizzard Award for RC in 2006 was to increase the effectiveness of undergraduate student learning by providing a program centered on explicit learning outcomes.

> These learning outcomes identify what students should be able to do by the completion of their undergraduate study. ... Using the learning outcomes, faculty and students engage one another in an open learning environment, where they question, discuss, and analyze real issues. The outcomes allow the College to deliver a seamless curriculum, where students' coursework, internships, co-curricular and extra-curricular activities, and personal lives interconnect. We believe outcomes-based learning at RC helps students to develop the skills, values, and beliefs necessary for leadership in the new millennium. (Zundel et al. 2006, 6f.)

The focus of this project also demonstrates RC's strong emphasis on outcomes and improved student learning, which was continued through many SoTL projects between 2007 and 2014 that addressed outcome-based design, learning, and assessment (Mengel, 2014, 2010b, 2008; Valk and Mengel 2007; Zundel and Mengel 2007). These and other projects (Couturier and Mengel, 2008; Kuruganti and Zundel, 2004) also repeatedly presented evidence for improved student learning in various learning outcomes; the improvements are captured and demonstrated by significantly higher student performance in the course-specific learning outcomes.

SoTL as Part of RC's Vision, Values, and Purpose.   Reviewing the role of the scholarship and practice of teaching and learning for RC was a major objective for the project of identifying RC's vision, values, and purpose in the academic year 2005–2006. Further, this project aimed at focusing the educational efforts and at increasing the accountability of RC (Collins and Porras 1991; Stewart and Carpenter-Hubin 2001).

The first and foremost result of the college's vision-strategy project engaging faculty, staff, students, and community leaders in and around Renaissance College in the process was the creation of the values, purpose, and strategic objectives of the college that guide its engagement in SoTL. In particular, the college has committed to experimenting with and modeling highly effective, innovative teaching and learning practices, and to improving postsecondary education by engaging in SoTL (Renaissance College 2006a, 2006b).

New Directions for Teaching and Learning • DOI: 10.1002/tl

As a first step, RC integrators published a model of curricular evolution and assessment demonstrating how SoTL "is an essential component in informing, guiding, and enabling the process of curricular evolution," thus contributing to the discussion of "new directions in teaching and learning" on a national and an international level (Zundel and Mengel 2007, 70). For example, the model of curricular evolution and assessment has informed quality assurance processes at Ontario universities and the development of international guidelines for leadership education programs (Ontario Universities n.d.; Ritch and Mengel 2009).

RC's Academic Plan and the Reality of the Economic Downturn in 2008. RC's commitment to SoTL both at RC and in the context of the larger scholarly community at UNB was clearly expressed in its academic plan for 2008, which also addressed RC's potential contribution to overall UNB priorities. In particular, RC committed to translating its lessons learned

> Into tools and practices that can be scaled up and transferred to different contexts (e.g., professional programs, larger first year service courses), by continuing to develop joint faculty positions, joint research projects and activities (e.g., working on effective tracking systems for learning outcomes). It is a major strategic importance that RC increase in its ability to help provide new models and tools for the University to improve its teaching and learning. ... We hope to continue to focus some of our SoTL work this year on this idea of transfer of RC's experience to other units. (Renaissance College 2008)

Unfortunately, the economic downturn of 2008 also heavily affected UNB and RC; in particular, faculty resources at UNB became increasingly scarce and the model of seconding faculty members to RC proved no longer viable. Due to the very small size of RC, cuts to its budget pushed RC into survival mode for the next four years. Engagement in SoTL could no longer be maintained and supported at a college level. Some RC employees, however, were able to contribute to SoTL individually at a reduced level even between 2008 and 2012; these contributions helped improve student learning and inform the discussion on local, national, and international levels, particularly in the fields of leadership and project management education (for example, Couturier and Mengel 2008; Mengel 2014, 2010a, 2010c, 2008; Thomas and Mengel 2014).

UNB's Task Force on RC in 2012. In order to formally assess the status of RC and to prepare a decision about its future, a vice presidential task force was created. It was tasked with reviewing RC's mandate and its effectiveness in contributing to the strategic goals of the university and its contributions to the learning culture at UNB and to SoTL in general. The task force collected comprehensive information, interviewed a wide range of stakeholders, and compiled a comprehensive report. The report included a key recommendation encouraging RC to formalize an SoTL-related research agenda and to become more active in contributing the results of their pedagogical innovations to the larger UNB community and to disseminate "the results locally, nationally, and internationally" (University of New Brunswick 2012, ii).

While the results of the task force were reported back to UNB and RC in May 2012, RC continued to be challenged by a scarcity of resources, and considerations about implementing some of the task force recommendations did not start before the fall of 2012. Individual work on SoTL, however, did continue, and results were presented (for example, Needham 2012).

Further systematic expansion of RC's work on SoTL was also halted by the ongoing internal search for the dean of RC between the fall of 2012 and June 2013. On July 1, 2013, a new dean of RC was appointed for a five-year term, which created the much-awaited security for RC. This stabilized context allowed the college to move forward with systematically addressing the issues and recommendations as identified in the task force report. At first, RC was able to successfully hire (August 1, 2014) a new full-time faculty member, which will significantly help release the strain on existing faculty and enable RC to make SoTL a priority at the college level.

Summary and Outlook

During the first eight years of RC, its faculty was able to make a significant contribution to SoTL on various levels. Individual and joint efforts on projects, particularly around learning outcomes and assessment, have resulted in numerous publications and in evidence for improved student learning. Shortcomings in terms of strengthening the impact on teaching at other units at UNB were identified and addressed in the strategic plan of 2008; however, the budgetary challenges starting in 2008 resulted in a shift of priorities toward the bare survival of RC's programs and put joint efforts on and a systematic approach toward SoTL on RC's backburner. The recommendations of the 2012 RC task force and the implementation of first steps have resulted in strong support for RC, somewhat stabilized its further development, and may provide opportunities for strategic involvement in SoTL.

The case study of RC provides lessons learned that might inform the development of SoTL in higher education in general:

- Institutional frameworks encouraging and supporting faculty involvement in SoTL, particularly including a tenure and promotion process that recognizes the significance of SoTL, can go a long way in motivating individual scholars and teams to focus a major part of their time and resources in this area.
- Engagement in SoTL projects focusing on outcomes and assessment improves student learning and can provide evidence for these improvements at the same time.

New Directions for Teaching and Learning • DOI: 10.1002/tl

- Budgetary constraints resulting in an only secondary focus on SoTL at an institutional level may indicate that SoTL is considered a stepchild of scholarly work; as a result, engagement in SoTL is left to individuals' interests and projects.
- Exposure of students, faculty, and administrators to and engagement with SoTL, even at a local faculty level, can function as a catalyst and contribute to the growth of SoTL and, ultimately, to improved student learning at a national level.

RC has a couple of challenges to master in the context of SoTL. In particular, our class sizes are growing. In continuation of RC's intent to work on innovative and effective teaching, faculty members are currently exploring new teaching approaches that allow welcoming more students into class, while maintaining the inquisitive, reflective, conversational, and experiential approach to learning. In general, various pedagogical elements of RC's programs (for example, learning outcomes, assessment, and engagement in various undergraduate and graduate programs) need to be reviewed and potentially innovated. Now may be a good time to review SoTL practice and establish a more systematic strategy considering the recommendations of the 2012 RC task force. The fact that faculty engagement in SoTL improves student learning locally and that it does have positive long-term effects on much larger levels encourages the continuation of RC's commitment to SoTL.

References

Collins, James C., and Jerry I. Porras. 1991. "Organizational Vision and Visionary Organizations." *California Management Review* 34(1): 30–52.

Couturier, Christian, and Thomas Mengel. 2008. "Mental Models in Youth Leadership Studies." *Academic Exchange Quarterly* 12(2): 195–199.

Kuruganti, Usha, and Pierre E. Zundel. 2004. "Teaching Quantitative Skills Using Repeated Problem-Solving Exercises Combined with Explicit Learning Outcomes." *Proceedings of The Atlantic Association of Universities 2003*, Atlantic Teaching Showcase, Dalhousie University, Halifax.

Mengel, Thomas. 2014. "'I love to study!' ... 'Well, I don't!'—Assessment of Student Motivation and Learning." *Proceedings of The Atlantic Association of Universities 2013*, Atlantic Teaching Showcase, Mount Allison University, Sackville, 96–109.

____. 2010a. "Getting Hooked Early On—Motivating Student Learning in First Year Courses and Beyond." *Proceedings of The Atlantic Association of Universities 2009*, Atlantic Teaching Showcase, Acadia University, Wolfville, 69–77.

____. 2010b. "Learning That Matters—Discovery of Meaning and Development of Wisdom in Undergraduate Education." *Collected Essays on Learning and Teaching (CELT) III*: 119–123.

____. 2010c. "Motivation 2.0: The Existential and Motivational Analysis—Engaging Students in Meaningful Leadership Learning." Conference proceedings of the global conference of the International Leadership Association. Boston.

___. 2008. "Preparing Leaders for Project Management—An Outcome-Based Approach to Leadership and Project Management Education." *International Journal of Project Management* 26: 275–285.

___. 2006a. "Leading into the Future?—A Review of Renaissance College's Leadership Curriculum." In *Proceedings of The Atlantic Association of Universities 2005*, edited by J. Hoyle, P. Nelson, and N. L. Pitts N. L. Nova Scotia Agricultural College, Truro: 177–193.

___. 2006b. "Values and Voices at Renaissance College: The Story of the Vision Quest and Learning Journey at UNB's Leadership School." In *Atlantic Universities' Teaching Showcase 2006. Proceedings of The Atlantic Association of Universities 2006*, edited by A. Hajek and E. Noseworthy. Memorial University of Newfoundland, St. John's, 69–87.

Mengel, Thomas, Terry Haggerty, Moon V. Joyce, and John Valk. 2006. "Teaching and Learning at the Crossroads—Renaissance College's (UNB) Undergraduate Degree Program in Interdisciplinary Leadership Studies." *Proceedings of the 8th Annual Conference of the International Leadership Association.*

Needham, Ted. 2012, October 15. "Learning and Assessing Social Interaction." Presentation at the 2012 AAU Teaching Showcase conference. University of New Brunswick/St. Thomas University, Fredericton.

Ontario Universities. n.d. Curriculum Design References and Resources. Accessed December 27, 2014. Available at http://oucqa.ca/guide/curriculum-design-references-and-resources/

Renaissance College. 2008. *Academic Plan.* Unpublished document.

Renaissance College. 2006a. "Core Values." Available at www.unb.ca/fredericton/renaissance/currentstudents/values.html

Renaissance College. 2006b. *Vision and Strategy of Renaissance College.* Unpublished document approved by RC Council.

Ritch, Steven, and Thomas Mengel. 2009. "Guiding Questions: Guidelines for Leadership Education Programs." *Journal of Leadership Education* 8(1): 216–227.

Stewart, Alice C., and Julie Carpenter-Hubin. 2001. "The Balanced Scorecard—Beyond Reports and Rankings." *Planning for Higher Education* (Winter): 37–42.

Thomas, Janice, and Thomas Mengel. 2014. "Preparing Project Managers to Deal with Complexity—Advanced Project Management Education." *Engineering Management Review, IEEE* 42(1): 57–72.

University of New Brunswick. 2012. *Task Force Renaissance College.* Unpublished report.

Valk, John, and Thomas Mengel. 2007, October 31. "Knowing Self and Others: Sustainable Leadership Education." Peer-reviewed presentation at the International Leadership Association Global Conference, Vancouver. *ILA Conference Proceedings.*

Zundel, Pierre, and Thomas Mengel. 2007. "The University of New Brunswick's Renaissance College: Curricular Evolution and Assessment at the Faculty Level." *New Directions for Teaching and Learning* 112: 69–82.

Zundel, Pierre, Mark Bishop, Micheal Carr, Gerry Clarke, Jo Anne Colford, Thomas Mengel et al. 2006. "Outcomes-Based Learning at a Whole Program Level." Award winning paper for the 2006 Alan Blizzard Award. Society of Teaching and Learning in Higher Education (STLHE). Retrieved from www.mcmaster.ca/stlhe/awards/2006%20Blizzard%20UNB.pdf

Thomas Mengel is a professor of leadership studies and integrator at Renaissance College, University of New Brunswick.

5

This chapter describes three research-informed SoTL initiatives undertaken at the McMaster Institute for Innovation and Excellence in Teaching and Learning and presents preliminary evidence of their impact on teaching, learning, and SoTL.

Developing the Scholarship of Teaching and Learning at the McMaster Institute for Innovation and Excellence in Teaching and Learning

Elizabeth Marquis, Arshad Ahmad

In 2013, McMaster University transformed the Centre for Leadership in Learning (CLL) into the McMaster Institute for Innovation and Excellence in Teaching and Learning (MIIETL). Like many SoTL institutes, this new unit was intended to enhance the university's contributions to pedagogical scholarship while still maintaining the existing support for teaching and learning provided by the CLL. Given that the creation of institutes devoted to the Scholarship of Teaching and Learning (SoTL) has been positioned as an effective means of integrating SoTL into institutional cultures (Poole, Taylor, and Thompson 2007), the creation of MIIETL generated a compelling opportunity to further enhance the impact of teaching and learning inquiry on our campus. In addition to signifying the kind of high-level institutional commitment that many think is necessary to grow and sustain SoTL (Ginsberg and Bernstein 2011), MIIETL also had the potential to facilitate connections between and among scholars, enabling interdisciplinarity and collaborative research (Boardman and Corley 2008) and contributing to the development of a community of champions who provide ongoing support for SoTL throughout the institution (Hubball, Clarke, and Poole 2010).

In spite of these promising possibilities, we remained aware that there currently exists little published evidence of the efficacy of SoTL institutes or of particular features, programs, or activities associated with them (see Hubball, Clarke, and Poole 2010 for one example of such work). In light

NEW DIRECTIONS FOR TEACHING AND LEARNING, no. 146, Summer 2016 © 2016 Wiley Periodicals, Inc.
Published online in Wiley Online Library (wileyonlinelibrary.com) • DOI: 10.1002/tl.20186

of this gap, we undertook a study examining the design and the perceived benefits and limitations of SoTL institutes at research-intensive universities worldwide. The results of this work, which have been described more fully elsewhere (Marquis 2015), provided a foundation upon which the scholarship component of MIIETL is currently being built. In this chapter, we outline some the steps taken to develop MIIETL's SoTL portfolio in the institute's first year, and provide preliminary evidence of the impact of those choices. While the initiatives described have evolved considerably since this chapter was written in August 2014, we hope this discussion of our first year progress will provide a helpful indication of some of the possibilities for the early stages of developing a SoTL institute.

The Establishment of MIIETL Research Fellows

Earlier research (Marquis 2015) indicated that effective SoTL institutes work to bring together and support a diverse range of scholars, creating a community of practice that both enhances the work conducted and helps individuals advocate for it within institutional cultures that can be unsupportive of teaching and learning inquiry (Mighty 2013). Nonetheless, this research also pointed out that such communities can be difficult to develop and sustain, particularly given demands on scholars' time (Brew 2010) and the fact that SoTL is often not rewarded or recognized in considerations of career progress (Walker, Baepler, and Cohen 2008). To this end, one of our immediate priorities has been to develop means for scholars from across campus to become formally and informally associated with the institute and to develop a sense of belonging to the unit and commitment to its work as a result.

As a first step in this direction, we collaborated with departmental partners in 2013 to establish two new faculty positions with combined responsibilities to MIIETL and to academic departments on campus. These positions are housed within individual departments/programs, but they are jointly funded by two departments and MIIETL. The individuals holding these positions are responsible for teaching within the funding departments and for conducting SoTL work within MIIETL, with 33 to 50 percent of their time allotted to the latter. In each case, the home department oversees career progress and merit decisions with active input from MIIETL and from the other contributing department. The appointments were initially made for a period of three years to allow for assessment of their impact and feasibility, with the intent to explore more long-term possibilities should they prove successful.

By officially making SoTL a substantial and recognized portion of these individuals' work, we hoped that these positions would create space for teaching and learning inquiry within their academic workloads and afford such work a sense of priority and importance. In addition, because these new roles involve responsibilities to MIIETL and to departments, we believed they could facilitate further connections between these units, enhancing the institutional impact and relevance of SoTL work conducted at the institute as a result. To this end, the positions were intended to respond to established challenges such as the underprioritizing of SoTL (Walker, Baepler, and Cohen 2008) and the lack of awareness of or support for it in many academic departments (Mårtensson, Roxå, and Olsson 2011).

Approximately one year into the life of these positions, these possibilities are already beginning to be realized. Both individuals who hold these roles have conducted significant amounts of SoTL work since beginning in their new positions, collectively contributing thirteen teaching and learning presentations (either individually or as parts of teams) to local, national, or international conferences and symposia, and publishing or submitting for publication twelve SoTL articles and reports. Of course, some portion of this research would likely have taken place in absence of these positions, given that both individuals were active SoTL practitioners before starting their new roles. Nevertheless, by creating explicit expectations to produce high-quality teaching and learning research and affording time for such work, these new positions have certainly contributed to supporting this research output.

Moreover, these individuals have also helped to foster new connections between MIIETL and the departments in which they work, initiating SoTL projects based on departmental questions, integrating the results of their research into teaching and learning in their programs, helping MIIETL learn from departmental innovations, and contributing to the development of collaborative initiatives with the potential to enhance student learning in their respective areas. They took active roles in the arts and science program's recent program review, for instance, applying knowledge about quality enhancement learned from colleagues in MIIETL to facilitate a process of curriculum mapping and shared reflection in the program. Likewise, in response to questions from arts and science about how learning portfolios might be used to meet program goals, they are currently working with MIIETL staff and arts and science students to conduct research addressing this issue.

Over the course of their first year, both cross-appointees have also worked to incorporate the results of their own and others' research into the design or redesign of courses, including required first-year offerings and innovative, experiential courses for upper-year students. One chaired a campus-wide committee to develop a new interdisciplinary inquiry class initiated by and housed in arts and science, for instance, and worked with a student on a SoTL project that informed the development of this course. She is currently working with additional students and the course instructor to develop a follow-up study investigating the extent to which the course meets its stated goals, which will in turn be used to refine the course as necessary. Similarly, the other inaugural cross-appointee has conducted extensive research about developing geospatial literacy through blended learning and is at present applying this knowledge as part of a MIIETL–geography and earth sciences team that has received funding from the Ontario Ministry of Training, Colleges, and Universities to redevelop a large geography course as an online offering. By integrating SoTL into new initiatives within their programs in this way, and by contributing to scholarly assessments of those initiatives, these positions appear to be contributing to the integration of teaching and learning research and practice in some departments.

Encouraged by these early successes, we sought to create additional positions of this nature in 2014 and to formally name these positions MIIETL Research Fellows. While one of the original fellows (the first author of this chapter) moved into the position of acting associate director of research at MIIETL at this time, the second continued in his position and was joined by five additional fellows, each of whom had joint responsibilities to MIIETL and at least one academic program on campus. Further corroborating arguments about the potential impact of these positions, this expanded group has already begun a number of SoTL projects connected to major goals and projects within their departments, including recruitment and retention initiatives and the development of online courses. Nonetheless, in order to more fully explore the question of impact, we are currently developing a research project that will collect information from a range of stakeholders (including the fellows themselves) about the benefits, drawbacks, and outcomes of these positions. Should the results of this study corroborate the preliminary results reported here, we hope to create additional fellow positions in the future.

Engaging Students as Co-Inquirers

As another part of developing and sustaining the diverse community of scholars recommended by our previous research about SoTL institutes, we have also prioritized the inclusion of students as active members of MIIETL's research team. A wide body of recent literature has documented the value of engaging students as co-inquirers in teaching and learning scholarship (for example, Felten et al. 2013), pointing out that such partnerships can foster transformative learning for both students and those with whom they partner, enhance the work undertaken, and ultimately increase its impact (McKinney 2012; Werder and Otis 2010). Heeding such converging evidence, we have embarked on a number of initiatives to engage students in MIIETL's SoTL work.

As one example of this process, we established a new "student scholar" program in collaboration with the arts and science program as well as a new arts and science course that allows program students to engage in independent SoTL work under the supervision of MIIETL staff members. Leadership for these initiatives was provided by one of the original research fellows, providing a further example of the ways that such positions can enable collaborative relationships between MIIETL and academic departments.

The student scholar program employs several undergraduate students each year as members of institute project teams. Students work ten hours per week in MIIETL and are paid for their time. The program piloted in 2013–2014 with thirteen students representing levels one through four of the arts and science program. These students worked with institute staff on a wide range of projects, including research examining community-engaged education and accessibility and inclusion in teaching and learning. In all cases, our intent was to involve students as collaborators who helped shape the work in which they were involved rather than as research assistants brought in simply to complete specified tasks.

Amongst other outcomes, the first year of this program led to a number of SoTL presentations and publications coauthored by students, including three manuscripts that were submitted for publication and a panel presentation at the 2014 conference of the Society for Teaching and Learning in Higher Education. Likewise, by the end of their contracts, student scholars were proposing new research projects for MIIETL to explore in the future, and some had invited additional faculty to partner with them on teaching and learning initiatives. These outcomes in particular suggested that the program had the potential not only to produce quality SoTL work but also to increase its impact by ensuring relevance to student audiences and being disseminated, through them, to other members of the teaching and learning community.

To further explore the impact of this program, a group of students, faculty, and staff who participated in its first iteration initiated a qualitative research project exploring our experiences of partnering with one another on teaching and learning projects. The results of this work, which have been submitted for publication, are promising. Projects benefited considerably from student involvement, and participation positively impacted the ways in which students approached their education. Nonetheless, echoing some literature about student–faculty partnerships (Allin 2014), this study also underlined a number of challenges that attach to partnering (such as the difficulties of navigating traditional power structures) and generated several suggestions for refining the program moving forward. Many of these, including an enhanced application process that encourages students to articulate their goals for projects from the outset, have been incorporated into the program for 2014–2015. This initial research project has also been adapted and applied to other MIIETL initiatives designed to engage students in the institute's work. By such means, we intend to further enhance the capacity of these initiatives to develop meaningful partnerships that generate relevant SoTL work and positively impact teaching and learning culture at the institution. Moreover, in correspondence with the call issued by Felten and colleagues (2013), we also plan to expand and further diversify our partnership efforts so that a wider range of students have an opportunity to become involved with our work moving forward.

Developing Priority Areas for Institute Scholarship

A final choice we wish to discuss here is the strategic selection of research priorities for the institute in its early days. Like much existing literature (Poole, Taylor, and Thompson 2007; Schroeder 2007), the study we conducted to inform the development of MIIETL emphasized the potential value of aligning institute research with established institutional priorities or with other initiatives that might have considerable bang for their buck. Thus, while we are still in the process of working with our campus community and other partners to shape our long-term research foci, we nonetheless elected early on to target a few large-scale projects that would directly affect student learning in a widespread way.

For example, learning from initiatives such as the Top 25 Program at Miami University (Taylor et al. 2012), one of our initial strategies was to focus attention on first-year classes that enroll a large number of students. In partnership with several faculties across campus, we received funding to create new "foundations" courses, which are intended to help first-year students transition to university, learn about and select academic programs, and develop essential skills that will serve them throughout their academic careers. These courses are being developed collaboratively by MIIETL and the faculties, and will take research-informed approaches to pedagogies such as blended- and inquiry-based learning. The first two of the courses (in the faculties of science and social sciences) are running for the first time, on an optional basis, in 2014–2015. If successful, they will become mandatory for all incoming students in those faculties in subsequent years. Research projects (also conducted in collaboration with the faculties and involving student partners and research fellows) have simultaneously been designed to investigate the outcomes of these initial offerings, looking at the extent to which they help students develop foundational skills, select academic programs, and transition to university. These studies will provide evidence to assess the courses' efficacy and refine them moving forward. In this way, SoTL work conducted in partnership with the institute will have an immediate impact on faculty initiatives that affect a large number of McMaster students directly. By continuing to conduct such strategic projects moving forward, we hope to maintain and enhance the institutional impact of SoTL work conducted in the institute.

Conclusion

Just over a year into MIIETL's existence, we remain excited about the institute's potential to contribute to the production of high quality SoTL that is woven tightly into the fabric of McMaster's teaching and learning culture. While we still have work to do to realize this potential fully, the initial outcomes reported here are promising. By emphasizing partnership with departments, cross-appointed faculty, students, and others and codeveloping research priorities with members of our campus community, we have begun to establish impact and will aim to enhance this impact in future.

References

Allin, Linda. 2014. "Collaboration Between Staff and Students in the Scholarship of Teaching and Learning: The Potential and the Problems." *Teaching and Learning Inquiry* 2(1): 95–102.

Boardman, Craig, and Elizabeth A. Corley. 2008. "University Research Centers and the Composition of Research Collaborations." *Research Policy* 37(5): 900–913.

Brew, Angela. 2010. "Transforming Academic Practice through Scholarship." *International Journal for Academic Development* 15(2): 105–116.

Felten, P., Julianne Bagg, Michael Bumbry, Jennifer Hill, Karen Hornsby, Maria Pratt, and Saranne Weller. 2013. "A Call for Expanding Inclusive Student Engagement in SoTL." *Teaching and Learning Inquiry* 1(2): 63–74.

Ginsberg, Sarah M., and Jeffrey L. Bernstein. 2011. "Growing the Scholarship of Teaching and Learning through Institutional Culture Change." *Journal of the Scholarship of Teaching and Learning* 11(1), 1–12. Retrieved from http://josotl.indiana.edu/issue/view/166

Hubball, Harry, Anthony Clarke, and Gary Poole. 2010. "Ten-Year Reflections on Mentoring SoTL Research in a Research-Intensive University." *International Journal for Academic Development* 15(2): 117–129.

Marquis, Elizabeth. 2015. "Developing SoTL through Organized Scholarship Institutes." *Teaching and Learning Inquiry* 3(2): 19–36.

Mårtensson, Katarina, Torgny Roxå, and Thomas Olsson. 2011. "Developing a Quality Culture through the Scholarship of Teaching and Learning." *Higher Education Research and Development* 30(1): 51–62.

McKinney, Kathleen. 2012. "Making a Difference: Application of SoTL to Enhance Learning." *Journal of the Scholarship of Teaching and Learning* 12(1): 1–7. Retrieved from http://josotl.indiana.edu/issue/view/177

Mighty, Joy. 2013. "One Important Lesson I've Learned from My Involvement with SoTL." *Teaching and Learning Inquiry* 1(1): 113–116.

Poole, Gary, Lynn Taylor, and John Thompson. 2007. "Using the Scholarship of Teaching and Learning at Disciplinary, National and Institutional Levels to Strategically Improve the Quality of Post-Secondary Education." *International Journal for the Scholarship of Teaching and Learning* 1(2). Retrieved from http://digitalcommons.georgiasouthern.edu/ij-sotl/vol1/iss2/3/

Schroeder, Connie M. 2007. "Countering SoTL Marginalization: A Model for Integrating SoTL with Institutional Initiatives." *International Journal for the Scholarship of Teaching and Learning* 1(1). Retrieved from http://digitalcommons.georgiasouthern.edu/ij-sotl/vol1/iss1/15/

Taylor, Beverley A.P., Andrea I. Bakker, Marjorie Keeshan Nadler, Cecilia Shore, and Beth Dietz-Uhler. 2012. "Integrating Inquiry-Guided Learning Across the Curriculum: The Top 25 Project at Miami University." In *Inquiry-Guided Learning*, New Directions for Teaching and Learning, no.129, edited by Virginia S. Lee, 61–70. San Francisco, CA: Jossey-Bass.

Walker, J.D., Paul Baepler, and Brad Cohen. 2008. "The Scholarship of Teaching and Learning Paradox. Results Without Rewards." *College Teaching* 56(3): 183–189.
Werder, Carmen, and Megan M. Otis, eds. 2010. *Engaging Student Voices in the Study of Teaching and Learning*. Sterling, VA: Stylus.

ELIZABETH MARQUIS *is an assistant professor in the arts and science program at McMaster University and associate director (research) of MIIETL.*

ARSHAD AHMAD *is associate vice president, teaching and learning, at McMaster University and director of MIIETL.*

6

This chapter briefly describes the SoTL research development program and context at Mount Royal University, reports initial results from a study of the program's impact on participants' teaching and scholarly activities, and situates the findings regarding individual impact, department-level impact, institution-level impact, and discipline-level impact within the current literature and the Canadian context.

SoTL^2: Inquiring into the Impact of Inquiry

Janice Miller-Young, Michelle Yeo, Karen Manarin, Miriam Carey, Jim Zimmer

Engaging in the Scholarship of Teaching and Learning (SoTL) can have many benefits for faculty and their students. Studies have demonstrated shifts toward more student-centered teaching approaches (Kember 2002) and improvements in student learning (Trigwell 2013; Waterman, Weber, Pracht, Conway, Kunz, Evans, Hoffman, Smentkowski, and Starrett 2010). Scholars have also reported that engaging in SoTL has had positive impacts in areas outside of teaching, such as informing program assessment and assisting interdisciplinary work beyond the SoTL (Bennett and Dewar 2013). For these reasons, it is no surprise that many colleges and universities are supporting SoTL.

Mount Royal's approach to developing SoTL was inspired by the faculty learning community work of Cox (2004) and others and by the Carnegie Scholars initiative of the Carnegie Academy. Our Institute for SoTL was established in 2008, and its main SoTL development program, the Nexen Scholars Program, has operated annually since 2009. This chapter briefly describes the program and initial results from a study of its impact on scholars.

Background

In September 2009, almost 100 years after its inception, Mount Royal College became Mount Royal University (MRU). This seemingly simple change in name followed an extended period of transition that included the

NEW DIRECTIONS FOR TEACHING AND LEARNING, no. 146, Summer 2016 © 2016 Wiley Periodicals, Inc.
Published online in Wiley Online Library (wileyonlinelibrary.com) • DOI: 10.1002/tl.20187

development of baccalaureate degrees, design of a new general education (liberal studies) provision, creation of teaching-service and teaching-service-scholarship faculty roles, creation of tenure and promotion procedures and faculty rank, and articulation of institutional research priorities. During the latter stages of its transition, Mount Royal affirmed its commitment to teaching and learning by establishing the Institute for SoTL. High-level institutional support for SoTL has been critical to the institute's success. Such support is visible in tenure and promotion documents, the University's Strategic Research Plan (2012), and the most recent Academic Plan (2012). The strength and consistency of institutional support for SoTL at MRU has enabled the institute to make significant headway with its programming and initiatives and has energized successful fundraising efforts on its behalf.

Separate from our well-established teaching support center, the Institute for SoTL reflects an institutional appreciation of SoTL as research that is distinct from teaching-related professional development and scholarly teaching. Thus, the institute operates as a research center, encouraging and supporting SoTL inquiries, providing resources and coordinating initiatives, and building a culture of inquiry about teaching and learning. The institute is self-supporting, relying on grants, donations, and revenue generation to fund its work. It sponsors a range of programs and initiatives, including research and dissemination grants, conferences and events, community outreach, writing residencies, and the Nexen Scholars Program.

Program Description

The Nexen Scholars Program, developed by former institute director and Carnegie scholar Richard Gale, supports an annual cohort of scholars who develop individual research projects to be conducted in a fall semester course. The annual request for proposals defined SoTL as "research into student learning, conducted within one's own class, that is evidence based, peer reviewed, and publicly shared; it is the investigation of fine-grained on-the-ground student learning outcomes of particular pedagogies; systematic scholarly inquiry into whatever influences the learning process."

From 2009 to 2013, the program consisted of three 3-day, off-site residencies over the course of one year, with monthly meetings in between (see Figure 6.1). Residencies involved participants working on their specific projects and discussing them in small groups with help from facilitators; after the first year, most facilitators were scholars from previous cohorts. Upon acceptance to the program, scholars were awarded a $2,000 grant that they could use not only for research purposes but also for professional development initiatives. Upon completion of the program, they also had the opportunity to apply for "going public" travel awards and to attend an optional five-day writing residency.

NEW DIRECTIONS FOR TEACHING AND LEARNING • DOI: 10.1002/tl

Figure 6.1. Scholars Program Structure 2009–2013

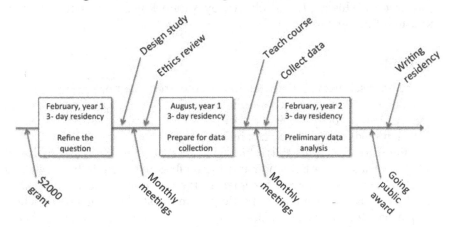

From 2009 to 2013, 41 full-time faculty members, eight contract faculty members, and one administrator participated in the program. Of these, six participants did not complete the program for reasons such as changes in teaching assignments or unexpected time constraints. Six scholars have also served in a facilitator role for subsequent cohorts. The impact of the program has not previously been systematically investigated; before this study, the only information collected was the number of travel grants given (33) and papers published to date (9).

Assessing Impact: The Study

Recognizing the many conceptualizations and purposes of SoTL, as well as the complexity of evaluating diverse and long-term outcomes, we took an open, inductive approach to investigating the impact of our program on its participants. We wanted to investigate whether the program has helped faculty meet their own goals for participation and whether it has influenced their teaching and scholarly activities. We also wanted to generate a baseline for more longitudinal studies and understand any issues that could inform the design of the program and other faculty development activities going forward both at Mount Royal and elsewhere.

Four authors of this chapter served as facilitators for different cohorts of Nexen Scholars and were the co-investigators for this study; three were also scholars in the first cohort and participants in the study. Therefore, the study methodology is a focused ethnography (Knoblauch 2005), in that the authors have a close familiarity and/or are members of the discrete community under investigation. Due to this familiarity, data collection can occur in short, intense phases, with the goal of understanding and describing social practices and inside perspectives (Higginbottom, Pillay, and Boadu 2013). Iterative, cyclic, and reflexive conversations amongst the co-investigator team occurred during the entire interview and data analysis process. This study was cleared by Mount Royal University's Human Research Ethics Board.

Methods

Twenty-five scholars participated in the study, the first phase of which consisted of an online survey asking about scholars' goals and the self-reported impact of the program. Survey responses were used to inform follow-up interviews, which were analyzed inductively.

Recruitment and Participants. Because our interests included scholars' goals for participation and their subsequent scholarly activity, all 50 MRU scholars who were accepted to the program in the years 2009 to 2013 were invited by e-mail to participate in the study. A total of 25 scholars participated, with 22 scholars completing an online survey and 17 being interviewed. Participants were distributed across cohort years and provided good representation across all faculties.

Data Collection. Initial evidence was gathered from a confidential online survey from January to March 2014. Adapted from Chick, Brame, and Wilsman (2013), the survey included five-point Likert-scale questions about how much impact scholars' projects and participation in the program had, as well as short-answer questions asking scholars to give supporting examples. The questions are summarized as follows:

- What were your goals for participating, and did you achieve them?
- Describe the study and outcome.
- How much impact did your project have on your teaching/subsequent scholarly activity? Explain.
- Do you continue to conduct SoTL investigations? Explain.
- Has participation in the Nexen program impacted your teaching/probability of pursuing subsequent SoTL projects/subsequent scholarly activity? Explain.
- Please describe your professional trajectory since participating in the program.

Scholars were also asked to participate in a follow-up interview. After reviewing the survey results for themes, we developed a semistructured interview protocol using the questions from the survey as a guide, with the purpose of getting more in-depth responses to the survey questions. Participants were given the opportunity to request a particular interviewer from the co-investigators, and all but one expressed no preference. For this reason, and so participants would feel free to speak as openly as possible, the investigator who had had the least involvement with the program conducted all but one interview. As the entire team of co-investigators met regularly over the period of the interviews to discuss emerging themes, we are confident this did not result in any inconsistency in the protocol. After 17 interviews, we felt we had reached data saturation as no new themes were emerging. All interviews were audio-recorded and transcribed. An initial thematic analysis was conducted separately by coresearchers and then discussed to reach consensus. Clear patterns emerged in this initial analysis; more detailed systematic analysis is ongoing.

Results

For the purposes of this chapter, we will summarize the survey results and emerging interview findings at a high level due to space constraints, with further work planned to delve into this rich data.

Survey Findings.   Participants most frequently reported goals related to developing their scholarship (40 percent), improving teaching (33 percent), and connecting with a community (20 percent). All but one said their original goals were met or exceeded. While less than half mentioned improved teaching as a goal, 89 percent rated the impact of the program on their teaching at 4 or 5 on the Likert scale; this is identical to the proportion who reported impact on scholarship.

Open-ended questions allowed participants to provide more detail about their experiences. Several interesting patterns emerged. The majority of participants wanted to learn more about the research process, including funding and publication opportunities; some wanted to establish a research plan in the area of teaching and learning. Some participants described conscious decisions to move away from their disciplinary research, while others described moving away from SoTL after the program. In describing impact on their teaching, participants noted increased attention to their roles as teachers and an increased intentionality in the consideration of pedagogical strategies and assessments. Some additionally noted a greater awareness of students' needs.

Interview Findings.   The semistructured interviews probed these areas of influence more deeply. We also began to see four kinds of impact emerge and began to ask questions regarding individual, department-level, institution-level, and discipline-level impact.

Interview themes served to confirm or explain the survey findings. For example, at the individual level, while more participants identified a research goal rather than a teaching-focused goal for their participation in the program, participation changed their teaching practices. As one participant said,

> I didn't even think of it impacting my teaching and so I was quite surprised when it did. Especially since it made me re-examine a lot of my different assumptions around my discipline and around my students, and it challenged some of my deficit narratives [about what students can't do] ... and it started me focusing more on what they were doing, rather than just my assumptions about what they could or couldn't do.

New Directions for Teaching and Learning • DOI: 10.1002/tl

Three things stand out in this response: (1) the underlying assumption going into the program that research on teaching is different from teaching, (2) the uncomfortable recognition of complicity in students' difficulties, and (3) an impact on teaching that goes beyond any single SoTL project. Many interviews describe variations of these elements, whether or not the participants were currently engaged in SoTL research. One participant, no longer involved in SoTL research, described a long-term impact on her teaching and her students:

> It has increased my interest in the scholarship of teaching and learning more broadly; so even though the project itself didn't do what I wanted it to do, understanding that there is a field out there and there are a lot of things that happen in that field has encouraged me to be more engaged in what is going on. So it has changed my understanding of how students learn, but also how I teach right now and why I teach the way I do.

Program impact extends far beyond specific publications arising from the program even as the desire for publication was one of the main reasons participants applied in the first place.

One emergent pattern that may have implications for the development of and recruitment into SoTL programs is the relationship between time at institution and area of impact. Participants who were relatively new to the institution tended to talk about impact, whether on their scholarship, their teaching, or their career paths in individual terms, while participants who had been at the institution for a longer period tended to talk about their departments, the institution, or their disciplines more often. We do not claim that participants were able to impact the institution or discipline at a broader level, but simply that this was how participants tended to frame their narratives.

This framing echoes, in some ways, the macro/meso/micro model of institutional culture as described in Williams et al. (2013) and elaborated in this volume by Verwoord and Poole, whereas Timmermans and Ellis, also in this volume, describe the contextual spheres of influence and impact. They argue for reciprocal relationships among individual, department, institution, and community within a SoTL system. Here we have individuals describing their spheres of potential impact from multiple positions, depending in part on length of time at the institution. Length of time may indicate career stage, level of security as represented through tenure, and institutional or disciplinary networks outside of the SoTL context.

This pattern has implications for recruitment into a SoTL program depending on the institutional objectives. Participants relatively new to the institution described the program as a way to meet other people and learn about the institution; participants who had been at the institution for a longer time described the program as a way to shape the institution. They talked about having the connections and being visible enough to make a difference: "I am a believer in SoTL and I think sometimes people listen to me because I have been around a while, making a pretty public stand going into SoTL." This participant described her participation in terms of service to the institution and discipline. A SoTL program can be a way to acculturate individuals entering an institution; it can also be a way to change the culture of an institution. These two objectives, however, involve different populations who probably require different types of support.

Conclusion and Future Work

This chapter focused on the relationship between goals and impact in data collected from the first five years of the Nexen Scholars program at Mount Royal University. The preliminary data analysis suggests most participants noted their original desire for scholarly growth and experienced a perhaps unanticipated impact on their actual teaching practices. Additionally, a faculty member's engagement with SoTL may vary in relation to his or her career stage, as represented by the proxy of length of time at the institution.

This study has yielded rich information in terms of impacts at the individual, departmental, institutional, and community/disciplinary levels. Further analysis and dissemination will explore this more deeply, as well as several other avenues of inquiry. For example, we have not examined the types of support individuals require at different career stages. We also note that while SoTL can be transformational both at the level of teaching and the level of scholarship, participation in SoTL often leads to a sense of discomfort, though our participants attribute this discomfort to different factors. The means of transformation and the associated sources of discomfort will form important avenues of further investigation.

References

Bennett, Curtis, and Jacqueline Dewar. 2013. "SoTL and Interdisciplinary Encounters in the Study of Students' Understanding of Mathematical Proof." In *The Scholarship of Teaching and Learning in and Across the Disciplines*, edited by Kathleen McKinney, 54–73. Bloomington, IN: Indiana University Press.

Chick, Nancy L., Cynthia Brame, and Adam Wilsman. 2013. "SoTL Programs for Graduate Students: Characteristics and Impact." Paper presented at the 10th Annual Conference of the International Society for the Scholarship of Teaching and Learning, Raleigh, NC.

Cox, Milton D. 2004. "Introduction to Faculty Learning Communities." *New Directions for Teaching and Learning* 97: 5–24.

Higginbottom, Gina M. A., Jennifer J. Pillay, and Nana Y. Boadu. 2013. "Guidance on Performing Focused Ethnographies with an Emphasis on Healthcare Research." *The Qualitative Report* 18(17): 1–16.

Kember, David. 2002. "Long-term Outcomes of Educational Action Research Projects." *Educational Action Research* 10: 83–103.

Knoblauch, H. 2005. "Focused Ethnography." *Forum: Qualitative Social Research* 6(3). Retrieved from www.qualitative-research.net/index.php/fqs/article/view/20/43#gcit

New Directions for Teaching and Learning • DOI: 10.1002/tl

Trigwell, Keith. 2013. "Evidence of the Impact of Scholarship of Teaching and Learning Purposes." *Teaching and Learning Inquiry* 1(1): 95–105.

Waterman, Margaret, Janet Weber, Carl. Pracht, Kathleen Conway, David Kunz, Beverly Evans, Steven Hoffman, Brian Smentkowski, and David Starrett. 2010. "Preparing Scholars of Teaching and Learning Using a Model of Collaborative Peer Consulting and Action Research." *International Journal of Teaching and Learning in Higher Education* 22(2): 140–151.

Williams, Andrea L., Roselynn Verwoord, Theresa A. Beery, Helen Dalton, James McKinnon, Karen Strickland, Jessica Pace, and Gary Poole. 2013. "The Power of Social Networks: A Model for Weaving the Scholarship of Teaching and Learning into Institutional Culture." *Teaching & Learning Inquiry* 1(2): 49–62.

JANICE MILLER-YOUNG *has been a faculty member at Mount Royal University since 2002 and the director of the SoTL Institute since 2013.*

MICHELLE YEO *has been a faculty developer and faculty member in Mount Royal University's Academic Development Centre since 2007.*

KAREN MANARIN *teaches in the departments of English and general education at Mount Royal University.*

MIRIAM CAREY *has been teaching at Mount Royal since 2001, first in the Department of Policy Studies and, more recently, doing faculty development in a secondment to the Academic Development Centre.*

JIM ZIMMER *is the associate vice-president, teaching and learning at Mount Royal University and led the establishment of the SoTL Institute in 2008.*

NEW DIRECTIONS FOR TEACHING AND LEARNING • DOI: 10.1002/tl

This paper presents the results of a quantitative study that comprehensively assessed the level and extent to which the Scholarship of Teaching and Learning (SoTL) was being conducted amongst faculty and staff at the University of Saskatchewan, and identifies the barriers and challenges faced by SoTL practitioners.

Exploring the SoTL Landscape at the University of Saskatchewan

Brad Wuetherick, Stan Yu, Jim Greer

A consensus has formed within growing circles in academia that there is scholarly research to be done on teaching and learning, that the systematic creation of rigorous knowledge about teaching and learning is a crucial prerequisite to responding to major challenges facing academia, that this knowledge must be shared publicly and should build cumulatively over time, and that the explorations of this area should be conducted by academics from all disciplines, not just those with appointments in schools of education. (Pace 2004, 1174)

The Scholarship of Teaching and Learning (SoTL), which has been defined as the "systematic study of teaching and/or learning and the public sharing and review of such work through presentations, performance, or publications" (McKinney 2006, 39) has grown more common as an aspect of scholarly work at many Canadian universities and at universities around the world (Hutchings, Huber, and Ciccone 2011). The vision articulated by Pace (2004), in which faculty across the disciplines are engaged in the "scholarly research (that needs) to be done on teaching and learning," has strongly influenced the vision for how SoTL is supported and developed

An earlier version of this paper was published in the April 2013 issue of *Bridges*, the U of S scholarly newsletter published by the Gwenna Moss Centre for Teaching Effectiveness (GMCTE). A full copy of the final report submitted to the Office of the Vice President Research; the Research, Scholarly, and Artistic Works Committee of Council; and the Teaching and Learning Committee of Council is available on the GMCTE website, www.usask.ca/gmcte.

at the University of Saskatchewan (U of S) (McDougall 2013; University of Saskatchewan 2008). Indeed, among the leadership group responsible for championing teaching and learning at the U of S (which includes, among others, the vice provost of teaching and learning, the director of Student Learning Services (formerly the University Learning Centre), the director of the Centre for Discovery in Learning, the chair of the Teaching and Learning Committee of Council, and the program director of the GMCTE), there was a sense that an increasing proportion of the entire campus community has been actively involved in the systematic creation and dissemination of knowledge about teaching and learning.

As strategic conversations were occurring about how to advance and enhance SoTL, including discussions within both the Research Committee and the Teaching and Learning Committee of University Council, a few key questions arose: How widespread is the scholarship of teaching and learning across the U of S campus? What is the extent (depth and intensity) of that scholarly research? How might SoTL be further supported at the U of S to extend the impact and reach of this work in the future?

In the summer of 2012, the GMCTE at the U of S, with support from the Office of the Vice President of Research, undertook a study to assess the level and extent to which SoTL was actively being conducted among U of S faculty and staff. The study also sought to categorize the depth and intensity of SoTL activity by examining the role of reflection and use of the literature in personal teaching practice (Glassick, Huber, and Maeroff 1997; Shulman 1987) and scholarly work related to teaching and learning (Prosser and Trigwell 2001; Trigwell, Martin, Benjamin, and Prosser 2000); to identify the barriers and challenges faced by SoTL practitioners; and to draw on the existing literature (Hutchings, Huber, and Ciccone 2011) to identify best practices for supporting this type of scholarship at the institutional level.

Using a snowball sampling technique, whereby deans, department heads, teaching award recipients, and known scholars of teaching and learning helped to identify other people in their faculty or department who were engaged in SoTL work, we identified a campus-wide SoTL community of 284 individuals, spanning every college and school within the institution and consisting of 247 faculty and 37 academic staff members. This number of individuals engaged in scholarly work on teaching and learning at a university with roughly 1,000 total faculty members exceeded expectations and estimates in advance of this study.

A 31-question electronic questionnaire, developed by the GMCTE, was administered to the cohort of identified faculty and staff members with a 70 percent response rate (198 respondents). Here we present some key findings from the study, which provide a snapshot of SoTL activity at the U of S—namely, the level, range, and type of activity; the sources and types of support currently available; and the extent to which SoTL activity can be said to be university-wide.

**Table 7.1. The SoTL Community at
the U of S by Academic Appointment**

Academic Appointment	Percentage
Full Professors	25%
Associate Professors	28%
Assistant Professors	23%
Staff	13%
Lecturers	5%
Sessional Teachers	5%
Teaching Stream Faculty	1%

The SoTL Community at the University of Saskatchewan

The identified U of S SoTL community is distributed across all types of academic appointment and across all disciplinary groups, as shown in Tables 7.1 and 7.2

For most faculty respondents (47 percent), their work in SoTL comprises less than one quarter of their scholarly work, while 18 percent indicated that SoTL constitutes more than three-quarters of their scholarly research effort. Although half of the faculty respondents indicated that this proportion has not changed over time, 41 percent reported that they now spend more time on SoTL than they had in the past. Only 27 percent of faculty respondents indicated that their SoTL projects are undertaken collaboratively more than half the time, while 81 percent of academic staff respondents reported that their SoTL projects are collaborative more than half the time. In addition, 49 percent of faculty and 41 percent of staff respondents indicated that their projects were multidisciplinary in that their collaborators were individuals from outside their own disciplines (including possibly outside of the institution).

A small subset of 23 faculty respondents also voluntarily submitted a CV for further analysis. The results of the CV analysis revealed that this subset of faculty had published 96 scholarly articles, book chapters, and books on their SoTL research, and since 2000 they had presented 224 SoTL-related

Table 7.2. The SoTL Community at the U of S by Disciplinary Group

Disciplinary Group	Percentage
Professional Social Sciences (Business, Education, Law)	22%
Health Sciences (Medicine, Nursing, Pharmacy and Nutrition, Kinesiology, Vet Med)	18%
Natural and Applied Sciences (Division of Sciences in Arts and Science, Engineering, Agriculture/Bioresources)	14%
Division of Social Sciences in Arts and Science	12%
Division of Humanities and Fine Arts in Arts and Science	12%
Academic Staff Respondents (Primarily from Student Services, the GMCTE, the Learning Centre, and Learning Technologies)	13%

NEW DIRECTIONS FOR TEACHING AND LEARNING • DOI: 10.1002/tl

Figure 7.1. The Extent to Which Respondents Feel That Involvement in SoTL is Visible to Departmental Colleagues (Five Item Scale—1 Invisible to 5 Highly Visible)

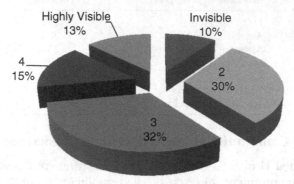

presentations at disciplinary or general teaching and learning conferences. Furthermore, we were able to identify that these individuals received over $1 million in research funding to conduct research on teaching and learning, with most of these grants coming from sources external to the U of S.

Overall, these findings suggest a larger-than-expected community of active SoTL researchers at the U of S, consisting of representation across disciplinary affiliation and a balanced distribution across professorial ranks, and one that is quite active and reasonably well networked across the campus and beyond. The survey results further reveal that the vast majority of faculty respondents demonstrate the primary characteristics of SoTL inquiry, namely critically reflecting on their teaching and reading the academic literature on teaching and learning. Moreover, the quantity of U of S scholars engaged in SoTL, as well as their level of engagement with SoTL, is increasing, with a substantial amount of scholarship being conducted in a collaborative and multidisciplinary fashion.

Barriers and Challenges

Previous work has shown that the visibility of SoTL work within faculty members' home departments has implications for the degree to which individuals conducting SoTL feel recognized and supported by their respective departments and institutions (Huber and Hutchings 2005; McKinney 2006). As seen in Figure 7.1, our survey found that only 28 percent of faculty respondents felt that their involvement in SoTL is visible to their departmental colleagues, while 40 percent felt that their work in SoTL has little to no visibility to their colleagues.

This lack of perceived visibility of SoTL work in academic departments has been found to be related to two other factors affecting the SoTL practice: (1) the perceived barriers to doing SoTL work and (2) the perceived legitimacy of SoTL work (Huber and Hutchings 2005; McKinney 2006).

NEW DIRECTIONS FOR TEACHING AND LEARNING • DOI: 10.1002/tl

Faculty were asked to respond to two open-ended questions. The first asked them to identify any barriers, challenges, or concerns that have stemmed from their involvement in SoTL; the second gauged their opinion on whether their research, scholarly, or artistic work on teaching and learning is perceived to have legitimacy as a form of scholarship according to policies and standards of their respective departments.

Of the 122 open-ended responses received, 38 percent of respondents cited that the lack of perceived legitimacy for their SoTL work was the primary barrier facing SoTL practitioners. Specifically, several faculty members commented that their work on SoTL is not recognized as a "real" form of scholarship by their departments, and when it is recognized, it is often relegated to the status of a "soft" or "fluffy" publication or "secondary" or "sideline" research and is valued much less than traditional disciplinary research.

A further barrier identified by many respondents is that their contributions in SoTL are neither recognized nor considered in their case for merit, promotion, or tenure, echoing the "visibility" and "legitimacy" findings described previously. Consequently, this works to discourage respondents' desire to actively pursue this type of scholarship. A third commonly indicated barrier was lack of time and difficulty balancing one's work in SoTL with other teaching, disciplinary research, and administrative obligations and responsibilities.

While the open-ended responses revealed that the failure to recognize SoTL as "real" scholarship was deemed as a barrier for nearly two-fifths of faculty, the remaining respondents felt in varying degrees that their departments recognize and value SoTL as a legitimate form of scholarship. Of these respondents, some noted further that the legitimization of SoTL has been a more recent development in their departments, whereas some stated that this degree of legitimacy remains contingent upon whether their work is published in high impact peer-reviewed venues or not. While reported challenges are pervasive and substantial, there is some indication to suggest, through the increased participation in SoTL throughout the academic community and through the inclusion of language around SoTL as an aspect of faculty evaluation, tenure and promotion, and institutional teaching award criteria, that the legitimacy and visibility barriers affecting SoTL work are beginning to shift at the U of S.

Best Practices to Support the Scholarship of Teaching and Learning Institutionally

Hutchings, Huber, and Ciccone (2011) identified a number of key practices for supporting SoTL at the institutional level:

- Understand, communicate, and promote an integrated vision of SoTL.
- Support a wide range of opportunities to cultivate the skills and habits of inquiring into teaching and learning.

NEW DIRECTIONS FOR TEACHING AND LEARNING • DOI: 10.1002/tl

- Connect SoTL to larger, shared agendas for student learning and success.
- Foster exchange between the campus SoTL community and those responsible for institutional research and assessment.
- Work purposefully to bring faculty roles and rewards into alignment with a view of teaching as scholarly work.
- Take advantage of and engage with larger, increasingly international teaching commons.
- Develop a plan and timeline for integrating SoTL into campus culture and monitor progress.
- Recognize that institutionalization is a long-term process.

These strategies are designed to align the educational goals of the institution with the principles of the scholarship of teaching and learning. Rather than being strictly prescriptive, they offer a guide that can be tailored and adapted in ways that benefit each individual institution's priorities and culture.

The heterogeneous nature of the SoTL activity at the U of S has several implications for these strategies, particularly to understand, communicate, and promote an integrated vision of the scholarship of teaching and learning. The critical factor in the success of this vision seems to be the congruence between how administrators understand the nature and aims of the SoTL work being done and how the practitioners themselves understand it. A better grasp of the range of SoTL activity on campus, as attempted in this study, is essential if SoTL is to be advanced as a legitimate research practice and a recognized form of scholarship. Upon presenting the results of this study to the Research Committee of University Council on campus, the committee chair wrote:

> Simply put, good scholarship is good scholarship, and it should be considered as a contribution at the University of Saskatchewan based on its merits. . . .
> The Committee supports there being a greater understanding and acceptance of research in the scholarship of teaching, and the development of standards by which meritorious SoTL contributions can be properly recognized, and considered in collegial processes. (Stephen Urquhart, letter from Research, Scholarly, and Artistic Works Committee of Council regarding the Scholarship of Teaching and Learning to author, January 30, 2013)

This response can be seen as a bit of a breakthrough, as this committee represents the campus research establishment, which in the past seemed to place little value on SoTL research.

Ultimately, however, the purpose of our study is to further understand the SoTL landscape at the U of S, with the aim of understanding how and what can be done to support and advance SoTL as part of the broader research landscape on campus. Several of the institutional strategies identified by Hutchings, Huber, and Ciccone (2011) are already in place (with varied levels of success and at various stages of development) at the U of S. The

Centre for Discovery in Learning, a campus-wide research center dedicated to research on teaching and learning, and the GMCTE serve as focal points for many of these initiatives. Some of their activities focus on providing local dissemination venues, including *Bridges* (the U of S scholarly newsletter for teaching and learning) and an annual SoTL symposium (entering its fifth year). Both centers also offer workshops and short courses dedicated to furthering participants' understandings of research on teaching and learning.

Other departmental and college-level initiatives are in place to support research on teaching and learning as well, including the College of Nursing's Centre for the Advancement of the Study of Nursing and Interprofessional Education, the (formerly titled) Educational Support and Development unit in the College of Medicine, the Centre for the Advancement of Accounting Education in the Edward's School of Business, and the recently approved School for Professional Development in the College of Engineering.

Much of what has been achieved on campus to this point, however, has been realized with little sustained (base budgeted) support from the institution. In the past, small SoTL research grants have been financed when contingency funds became available, with strong responses to calls for proposals. A set of SoTL grants will be made available this year and, in partnership with the research office, they will be promoted and supported as part of the suite of internal research grants available to faculty. More recently, the university established a significant curriculum innovation fund, and also launched a major initiative in experiential learning. Both of these initiatives include funding to support program evaluation, with the potential for supporting departments or colleges to consider SoTL early on in their planning of a curriculum renewal or experiential learning project.

Starting this academic year, the GMCTE will be working to support the SoTL endeavors of a relatively new cohort of faculty members appointed in teaching-focused roles. Individuals in these roles will have an explicit expectation of engaging in SoTL as their scholarly work. It is hoped that working with them as a community will help to build capacity and foster a culture of peer support for SoTL work on campus. These new programs are showing promise for stimulating more SoTL activity. And while it is acknowledged that, in the words of Hutchings, Huber, and Ciccone (2011), institutionalization is a long-term process, the process is indeed underway at the U of S.

References

Glassick, Charles E., Mary Huber, and Gene I. Maeroff. 1997. *Scholarship Assessed: Evaluation of the Professoriate.* San Francisco, CA: Jossey-Bass.

Huber, Mary, and Patricia Hutchings. 2005. *The Advancement of Learning: Building the Teaching Commons.* San Francisco, CA: Jossey-Bass.

Hutchings, Patricia, Mary Huber, and Anthony Ciccone. 2011. *Scholarship of Teaching and Learning Reconsidered: Institutional Integration and Impact.* San Francisco, CA: Jossey-Bass.

McDougall, Patricia. 2013, April. "Scholarship of Teaching and Learning at the Heart of Academic Culture: Integration Doesn't Happen Overnight!" Keynote presentation at the Third Annual University of Saskatchewan SoTL Symposium, Saskatoon, SK.

McKinney, Kathleen. 2006. "Attitudinal and Structural Factors Contributing to Challenges in the Work of the Scholarship of Teaching and Learning." *New Directions for Institutional Research* 129(Summer): 37–50.

Pace, David. 2004. "The Amateur in the Operating Room: History and the Scholarship of Teaching and Learning." *The American Historical Review* 109(4): 1171–1192.

Prosser, Michael, and Keith Trigwell. 2001. *Understanding Teaching and Learning: The Experience in Higher Education*. Philadelphia: The Society for Research in Higher Education & Open University Press.

Shulman, Lee. 1987. "Knowledge and Teaching: Foundations of the New Reform." *Harvard Education Review* 57(1): 1–22.

Trigwell, Keith, Elaine Martin, Joan Benjamin, and Michael Prosser. 2000. "Scholarship of Teaching: A Model." *Higher Education Research & Development* 19(2): 155–168.

University of Saskatchewan. 2008. *Teaching and Learning Foundational Document*. Retrieved from www.usask.ca/ipa/documents/TLFD_Council_Approved_Version_December_2008.pdf

BRAD WUETHERICK is the executive director of learning and teaching in the Office of the Provost and vice president academic and Centre for Learning and Teaching at Dalhousie University.

STAN YU is a research associate with the International Centre for Northern Governance and Development and former research and program evaluation analyst with the Gwenna Moss Centre for Teaching Effectiveness at the University of Saskatchewan.

JIM GREER is a professor of computer science, senior strategist for learning analytics, and former director of the University Learning Centre at the University of Saskatchewan.

NEW DIRECTIONS FOR TEACHING AND LEARNING • DOI: 10.1002/tl

8

In this chapter, we reflect on and analyze the impact of a confluence of events that led us to reconceptualize our approach to supporting the Scholarship of Teaching and Learning at our institution.

Reconceptualizing the Scholarship of Teaching and Learning at the University of Waterloo: An Account of Influences and Impact

Julie A. Timmermans, Donna E. Ellis

Our focus in this chapter is introspective, examining the work of our teaching center in relation to the Scholarship of Teaching and Learning (SoTL). In 2011, we came to a crossroads in supporting, guiding, and leading the scholarship of teaching and learning at the University of Waterloo (UWaterloo). A confluence of events prompted us to reexamine and then reconceptualize our approach to this work. Our contribution to this volume is a reflective piece in which we analyze the impact of these events on our thinking and practice as an educational development unit and document our attempt to develop a contextually sensitive definition, conceptualization, and approach to supporting investigations into teaching and learning at our institution.

Establishing the Context

Educational development is a practice that is contextually situated (Sorcinelli, Austin, Eddy, and Beach 2006; Taylor and Rege Colet 2010). The multiple layered contexts in which SoTL is ensconced play a crucial role in shaping the approach and design of our work. To begin our analysis, we examine the various contexts that have had an impact on SoTL work at our institution.

General Institutional Context. The University of Waterloo is perhaps most renowned for its innovative and entrepreneurial nature. A research-intensive, comprehensive university in Southwestern Ontario, it has over 35,000 students and 1,100 faculty members across six faculties and

NEW DIRECTIONS FOR TEACHING AND LEARNING, no. 146, Summer 2016 © 2016 Wiley Periodicals, Inc.
Published online in Wiley Online Library (wileyonlinelibrary.com) • DOI: 10.1002/tl.20189

ten professional schools. Programs emphasize innovation and experiential education, with over half of all undergraduates participating in cooperative education programs.

The vision of our institution-wide teaching center, the Centre for Teaching Excellence (CTE), is "to inspire teaching excellence, innovation, and inquiry" (https://uwaterloo.ca/centre-for-teaching-excellence/about-cte). Our center has almost 30 people supporting its mission: a director (Donna), senior instructional developers, instructional developers (including Julie), liaisons for each of the faculties, an educational research associate, graduate instructional developers, TA workshop facilitators, and administrative staff. The CTE reports to the Office of the Associate Vice President, Academic, which in turn reports to the Office of the Vice President, Academic and Provost. SoTL work is supported by CTE staff, and the center receives funding from the senior administration for SoTL activities in addition to senior administrators' presence at and involvement in these activities.

Catalysts to a Shift in Approach

SoTL work has been supported on our campus since 1999. A confluence of events in 2011 resulted in a reconceptualization of how this work is now supported by our center.

A staffing change at CTE led us to reflect on how we had been approaching SoTL and might continue to do so. Since we had tried providing different types of support over time (for example, theme-based grants, data collection services, research methods workshops), this seemed an opportune time to solicit client feedback. A small-scale needs assessment about the work of the center revealed that while both benefits and challenges could be identified related to engaging in SoTL work, the drawbacks were significant obstacles. For example, faculty members who had engaged in SoTL perceived that awareness of and rewards for this type of research were limited across the institution, and they lacked confidence with the higher education literature and research methodologies that were typically not part of their disciplinary backgrounds. There was also a sense that the strong prevalence of STEM disciplines at UWaterloo created a context in which providing concrete strategies for learning how to teach more effectively was more valuable than an approach to promote the formation of social science researchers.

Concurrently, at the institutional level, a university-wide task force on innovative teaching practices to promote deep learning was struck and comprised members from all faculties, as well as from CTE. The final report included recommendations that the definition of and approaches to SoTL be more flexible. SoTL had been defined and promoted as engaging in doing research on teaching and learning, with the ultimate intent of public dissemination. The report authors called for an expansion of this definition, including a call to open up the scope of the existing annual teaching and learning conference, and the grant program to include the application of existing research and examples of best practices to promote faculty professional development around teaching and learning. In support of these revised activities, the faculty-based "teaching fellows" were launched "to provide leadership in teaching within their unit in order to develop a set of best practices for teaching which will improve the depth, effectiveness, and efficiency of student learning in their unit" (Ellis et al. 2011, 20–21).

At approximately the same time as these shifts, research funded by the Higher Education Quality Council of Ontario (HEQCO) indicated that the majority of faculty members were not conducting classroom research (Britnell et al. 2010, 57). Furthermore, only 18 percent were learning about teaching by conducting research on teaching, while 75 percent were learning about teaching by consulting with colleagues (Britnell et al. 2010, 21). While the authors of that report provided aspirational outcomes for increased support for traditional SoTL research, data about practices from the HEQCO report in conjunction with our institutional reality gave us pause about how best to proceed.

Reconceptualization Phase

The various events shared previously occasioned shifts in our conceptualization of and approach to SoTL. We now describe the principles that guide our revised approach—principles based on knowledge of our clients and their contexts.

We heard the need for more *flexibility* in how we guide, promote, and lead SoTL work. A flexible approach is consonant with two threshold concepts in the careers of educational developers (Timmermans 2014). In this study, experienced Canadian educational developers identified ideas that have transformed their ways of knowing and being during their careers. The notion of "starting where people are" was pivotal. With this principle, facilitating change or development begins with knowledge of the center's clients. We can benefit, for example, from knowing our clients' motivations, aspirations, and perhaps limitations. Rather than implementing a uniform view and approach, or pushing for an ideal that is too far beyond our clients' current state, a more flexible approach allows us to use knowledge of where people are as a departure point and beacon for moving forward.

This flexible approach also captures another core way of knowing and being named by educational developers, which is "understanding and adapting to context." With this approach, educational developers seek information about the various contexts in which clients are embedded, thereby knowing about context so that we may know in context. Such knowledge enables us to adapt to context and facilitate a process that is contextually specific and relevant. For us, knowing our clients' obstacles was critical in refocusing our efforts.

NEW DIRECTIONS FOR TEACHING AND LEARNING • DOI: 10.1002/tl

The impact of adopting these principles as foundations for our SoTL work has been significant: We have recognized the need to expand our vision of what would constitute SoTL at our university. Thus, from a vision of providing support for work that fits the traditional definition of SoTL—that is, one in which research is undertaken and is publicly disseminated (for example, Hutchings and Shulman 1999)—the center now provides support for the continuum of scholarly work on teaching and learning, from reflective practice to the more "traditional" forms of SoTL research. Furthermore, we have recognized that labels we put on practices can have the effect of inviting or alienating our clients from engaging in this important work. Our less frequent use of the term SoTL and more frequent use of the term *scholarly teaching* appears to render this work more accessible, inviting people who may not have previously felt welcome.

Finally, we are guided by the principle of *alignment*. In our work as educational developers, we often encourage people to strive for alignment among the outcomes, instructional strategies, and assessments in course design, for example. In reconceptualizing our approach to SoTL, we have refocused resources to align with supporting scholarly teaching.

Responding to the Influences of These Various Contexts

In this section, we describe three key shifts that we have made in an attempt to align our actions with our revised conceptions.

Staffing.   As a result of the events in 2011, the staff position at CTE supporting SoTL work was redesigned to support and promote faculty members' adoption of a scholarly approach to investigations into teaching and learning. This approach encourages drawing on and applying the pedagogical literature and showing evidence of reflection on teaching and learning (Bass 1999; Felder and Brent 2001). Prior to 2011, this position had been solely responsible for supporting SoTL; the revised position now has the dual role of consulting with clients on not only research on teaching and learning but also instructional practices, thereby demonstrating our commitment to both research and practice. The educational research associate (ERA) who supports this role no longer provides data collection or analysis services as the initial ERA did; rather, she assists Julie in consulting on educational research as well as supports center-wide assessment activities.

Grants.   CTE has been administering a centrally funded teaching and learning grants program since 2004. In 2012, the focus of these grants was expanded to include instructional development projects, and the Learning Innovation and Teaching Enhancement (LITE) Grants were launched. The purpose of the grants is to provide support for investigating student learning and alternative approaches to teaching and assessing learning at the individual, departmental, faculty, or institutional levels. The overall aims are to foster deep learning and to promote curiosity, reflection, and exploration in the areas of teaching and learning. Grant projects may focus on one or a combination of the following three themes: (1) assessing new approaches to teaching and learning (What is possible and does it work?); (2) critically examining student learning with existing instructional approaches (What is happening and what could be improved?); and (3) pursuing instructional development opportunities (How could I teach differently to better facilitate deep student learning?).

Our revised program consists of two types of LITE grants: seed grants, for one-year projects up to $5,000, and full grants for projects up to $30,000 over two years. Both grant formats emphasize the contribution of the projects to UWaterloo's learning community. There are now three annual application deadlines, as opposed to one, including two deadlines for seed grants and one for full grants. Applications are blind peer reviewed.

Since the inception of these grants in 2012, and at the time of writing this paper, over 50 projects from across all faculties have been funded. The range of project topics is rather remarkable and includes inquiries into online learning, experiential learning, case-based and community service learning, learning across disciplines, language learning, assessment, written communication, teamwork, and many more. One hundred forty unique individuals have been involved in a LITE Grant project. Most projects are collaborations within or across units. Several projects include graduate or undergraduate students as coapplicants. The LITE Grant website through CTE features descriptions of the projects, as well as provides a forum for sharing resources generated, such as reference lists and presentation materials.

After several rounds of receiving grant applications, we have come to realize that while ideas for projects abound, applicants are often at a loss when it comes to clearly defining the types of learning they are seeking to enhance and elaborating a valid means of assessing whether this learning has been achieved. This observation has led to two outcomes. The first is a realization that we need to give applicants more intentional support by providing resources and guidance with respect to defining learning (or conditions for learning), assessing the learning, and using these assessments as data for projects. This is a significant shift away from previous efforts to provide programming and support on research methodologies, but we hypothesize that greater clarity about the intent of scholarly teaching projects and explicit guidance on how to integrate existing course-related work into such projects will make the projects more manageable for our clients.

The second outcome has been a center-wide initiative to hold discussions and professional development sessions on theories of learning and assessment practices, so that we too can be reflective practitioners and examine the definitions of and assumptions about learning and assessment we bring to consultations. This initiative also builds capacity in the center, distributing among members the ability to support scholarly teaching work that is focused on defining and assessing student learning. These changes are consistent with the principles that helped us to reconceptualize our work, including the need to acknowledge where people are starting from and the UWaterloo context.

Annual Teaching and Learning Conference.   Since 2009, UWaterloo has hosted an annual teaching and learning conference that is organized by CTE and generously supported by the Office of the Associate Vice President, Academic, and the faculty association. In 2012, the scope of the conference changed to mirror the grants, and it thereby serves as a venue for sharing not only research but also best practices about teaching and learning. While colleagues from neighboring universities are welcome, the focus is on encouraging the UWaterloo community to attend, so that we may develop a local community and culture of professional development around teaching and learning.

One of the most popular conference sessions is our "Igniting Our Practice" session, which features short demonstrations of instructional practices used by our award-winning teachers. Introduced at the 2012 conference, attendees consistently comment that this is one of the most thought-provoking sessions of the day. One participant elaborated that the session had prompted him/her to "think about how their methods could translate into my discipline, and also be more open to alternative teaching methods." Having this plenary session in addition to an outside keynote speaker who shares research-based expertise on teaching and learning again demonstrates our commitment to valuing and promoting both research and practice. We are aligning our actions with our conceptions.

Contemplating Impacts

As we write this chapter, our center is in the midst of developing a comprehensive assessment plan for all of our areas of service. These efforts have allowed us to recognize that we have been collecting primarily *output* data in relation to our support of scholarly teaching work, such as number of grants awarded, number of grant holders, number of conference attendees, and so forth. Since revising our scholarly teaching initiatives, however, we have also put into place some data collection questions that will enable us to move toward assessing *outcome* data. For example, our report template for completed grants asks for a description of each project as well as the outcomes, dissemination, and perceived impact.

At some point, these reports could be qualitatively analyzed to determine impacts at different levels (for example, individual students and/or faculty members, the institution). These data, though, will not easily reveal more systemic shifts in our institution's pedagogical culture. For example, they will not likely tell us about tenure and promotion policies that are changed to explicitly encourage and count scholarly teaching research. Nor will they tell us about people's paths from hearing a research-based idea at our conference that leads them to apply for a LITE grant to study their implementation of that idea in a course. What are the most salient data to track as impacts? And what about the impact of scholarly teaching work on the unit that helps to support it? As we develop a plan for assessing the work of our center, these types of questions are foremost in our thoughts.

Conclusion

In this chapter, we have provided a case study of how our conceptions of and approach to supporting scholarly teaching evolved as a result of events within the University of Waterloo and our professional community. We reflected on historical documents and recollections to better understand our current state, and how we engage in the work of educational development, which for us includes supporting scholarly teaching research. If those who support such initiatives—however they may be defined—are key inputs to a system of pedagogical change, then perhaps it is valuable that the focus of analyzing the impact of these initiatives be turned not only outwardly but also inwardly. In our teaching center, we will continuously reflect on and study our support of research on scholarly teaching to ensure that we refine our approach and align this approach with our institutional context. This does not mean that we will not challenge that context, but we need to understand it, accept it, and work within it in order to influence it.

References

Bass, Randy. 1999. "The Scholarship of Teaching: What's the Problem?" *Inventio* 1(1): 1–10.

Britnell, Judy, Bettina Brockerhoff-Macdonald, Lorraine Carter, Debra Dawson, Leslie Doucet, Frederick Evers, Shirley Hall et al. 2010. *University Faculty Engagement in Teaching Development Activities Phase II*. Toronto: Higher Education Quality Council of Ontario.

Ellis, Donna, Carey Bissonnette, Steve Furino, Shirley Hall, Tim Kenyon, Ron McCarville, Gordon Stubley, and Clarence Woudsma. 2011. *The Task Force on Innovative Teaching Practices to Promote Deep Learning at the University of Waterloo: Final Report*. Retrieved from https://uwaterloo.ca/centre-for-teaching-excellence/sites/ca .centre-for-teaching-excellence/files/uploads/files/Task%20Force%20Report%20on%2 0Deep%20Learning_0.pdf

Felder, Richard M., and Rebecca Brent. 2001. "Effective Strategies for Cooperative Learning." *Journal of Cooperation & Collaboration in College Teaching* 10(2): 69–75.

Hutchings, Patricia, and Lee Shulman. 1999. "The Scholarship of Teaching: New Elaborations, New Developments." *Change* 31(5): 10–15. doi:10.1080/00091389909604218

Sorcinelli, Mary Deane, Ann Austin, Pamela Eddy, and Andrea Beach. 2006. *Creating the Future of Faculty Development: Learning From the Past, Understanding the Present*. Bolton, MA: Anker Publishing.

Taylor, K. Lynn, and Nicole Rege Colet. 2010. "Making the Shift from Faculty Development to Educational Development: A Conceptual Framework Grounded in Practice." In *Building Teaching Capacities in Higher Education: A Comprehensive International Model*, edited by Alenoush Saroyan and Mariane Frenay, 139–167. Sterling, VA: Stylus.

Timmermans, Julie. 2014. "Identifying Threshold Concepts in the Careers of Educational Developers." *International Journal for Academic Development* 19(4): 305–317. doi:10.1080/1360144X.2014.895731

JULIE A. TIMMERMANS *is an instructional developer at the Centre for Teaching Excellence at the University of Waterloo.*

DONNA E. ELLIS *is the director of the Centre for Teaching Excellence at the University of Waterloo.*

NEW DIRECTIONS FOR TEACHING AND LEARNING • DOI: 10.1002/tl

9

Drawing on the concepts of emergent and appointed leadership, this article expands on the role of social networks in SoTL (Roxå and Mårtensson 2009, 2012; Williams et al. 2013) by examining the nature of these networks, relationships between these networks, and support for them, in order to theorize how institutions can foster cultural change to support SoTL.

The Role of Small Significant Networks and Leadership in the Institutional Embedding of SoTL

Roselynn Verwoord, Gary Poole

Integrating the scholarship of teaching and learning (SoTL) into institutional cultures can encourage teaching improvement and a sustainable focus on student learning (Poole and Simmons 2013). Building on the work of Williams and colleagues (2013) that articulated a multilevel model for embedding SoTL institutionally, this chapter explores the role of social networks in SoTL by "zooming in" on the nature of these networks, the relationships between these networks, and support for them. We apply the concepts of emergent and appointed leadership at different institutional levels (micro, meso, and macro) in order to theorize how institutions can foster cultural change to support SoTL, particularly when the impetus for change often exists "backstage" (Roxå and Mårtensson 2009, 2012) in instructors' small significant networks. To illustrate the importance of these ideas in practice we: (1) highlight case studies involving individuals in various emergent and appointed leadership positions at micro, meso, and macro levels at the University of British Columbia (UBC), and (2) reflect on the development of our significant networks from our positions as appointed leader and developing leader at UBC, while emphasizing the values of generosity and service as well as the practice of mentoring.

NEW DIRECTIONS FOR TEACHING AND LEARNING, no. 146, Summer 2016 © 2016 Wiley Periodicals, Inc.
Published online in Wiley Online Library (wileyonlinelibrary.com) • DOI: 10.1002/tl.20190

Weaving SoTL into Institutional Cultures: The Williams et al. (2013) Model

Recognizing that it is a daunting task to change institutional cultures, Williams and colleagues (2013) used the metaphor of weaving to highlight the importance of bringing together the multiple and sometimes disparate threads that comprise institutional culture. Drawing on theories of networks and communities of practice (CoPs), they articulated a multilevel model (see Figure 9.1) to describe how networks and CoPs can operate within and among three levels (micro, meso, and macro) that are typical within most postsecondary institutions in Canada. The micro level represents the activities of individuals, the meso level represents middle management, and the macro level represents senior management. The arrows represent connections among individuals and networks, and the permeability of the levels and the dotted and solid lines indicate the ties (both strong and weak) that can develop between individuals and CoPs.

Figure 9.1. Williams et al. (2013) Model for Weaving SoTL into Institutional Cultures. (Material appears courtesy of Indiana University Press and Teaching & Learning Inquiry. All rights reserved.)

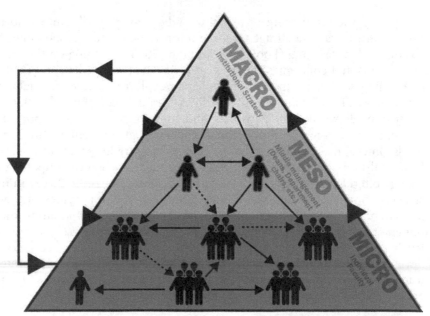

Macro Level: Sets the strategic direction
Meso Level: Interprets key issues and acts as conduit of information both upwards and down
Micro Level: Activities of communities of practice, individual faculty and students

Small Significant Networks and SoTL

In an effort to advance Williams and colleagues (2013) model, we draw on the work of Roxå and Mårtensson (2009, 2012), who examined the conversations that academic teachers (individuals engaging in teaching in higher education and whom we refer to as faculty members and instructors) have about teaching and how the effects of academic teacher training propagate into local contexts. They found that: (1) instructors form small significant networks (small, trusted, and private networks) with other individuals to discuss teaching and these networks influence instructors' practice, and (2) when academic cultures are supportive of SoTL, more conversations occur. This support emanates most importantly from those operating at the meso and macro levels. Although Roxå and Mårtensson (2009, 2012) adopt a cultural perspective that sees micro as individual work, meso as significant networks and workgroups, and macro as management, using their language, we adopt an organizational approach, seeing micro as rank and file instructors working along and in groups, meso as middle managers, and macro as senior administration.

We believe that these small significant networks are necessary for weaving SoTL into institutional cultures. We also speculate that cultures supportive of SoTL increase the likelihood that these conversations become more SoTL-like and scholarly. Although Roxå and Mårtensson do not discuss the possibility that the members of an instructor's network are strategically chosen to often confirm our views rather than expand them, we believe that it is at least as likely that these conversations reinforce the status quo and actually inhibit change. If this is true, how do institutions foster cultural change to support SoTL when the possibility for change occurs backstage (Roxå and Mårtensson 2009, 2012) in instructors' small significant networks? We believe one answer to this question lies in the dyadic interactions between "local leaders" at the meso level and those in micro-level networks.

The Importance of Dyadic Interactions

The Williams and colleagues' (2013) model features groups of people working in networks at the micro level and individuals in meso- and macro-level leadership positions. Most of the interactions in the model occur between pairs of people. This might be between two members of a network or between two people working across networks. The dyad might feature a power difference if one person is at the meso level and the other is at the micro level. Whatever the combination, when we zoom in on the model, we must be cognizant of the dynamics of dyadic interactions. One caution is that dyadic interactions must occur between networks and not just within them. Furthermore, leaders must communicate directly and effectively with individuals, rather than through blanket messages that one hopes will land in the right places. With this in mind, we now look closer at the nature of leadership that helps weave SoTL into institutional culture.

Working at the Meso Level: Emergent and Appointed leaders

When Mårtensson (2014) introduced the term *local leadership,* she provided a useful way of thinking about the activity at the meso level of the Williams and colleagues (2013) model. Mårtensson (2014) asserted that this form of leadership is essential to the success of micro-level networks. We agree and consider this local leadership to take both "appointed" and "emergent" forms (Hogan and Hogan 2002). The former depicts leadership based on an appointed position within an institution and is, therefore, a product of macro-level decision making. The role carries various expectations, possibly defined by a job description. Emergent leadership, in contrast, is more organic in nature. Emergent leaders might operate exclusively at the micro level, working as "hubs" that connect small significant networks. Alternatively, leaders may emerge from the micro level and move into the meso level. By serving in these capacities, they provide support, strength, and social capital (Burt 2000) for micro-level networks, enabling SoTL to flourish.

Emergent Leadership in Support of Small SoTL Networks.   Roxå and Mårtensson's (2009) small significant networks often form serendipitously, perhaps in hallways or lunchrooms. Social network analysis would predict that, over time, connections would develop *between* these networks, enriching their perspectives and providing sources of information. Between-network connections are facilitated by individuals (hubs) within the networks. Hubs have special skills and opportunities that allow for the bridging of gaps. Dawson, Tan, and McWilliam (2011, 928) call these network connectors "border crossers," describing them as people who possess "the enterprise and agility required for bridging the network gaps and introducing new knowledge, ideas, and processes to the larger network."

These positions provide venues for emergent leaders to champion SoTL through support of small networks. For example, when Niamh Kelly developed an online version of a course in pathology, she became interested in the nature of her students' learning in this environment. The ensuing research took her from "STEM (Science, Technology, Engineering, and Mathematics) to SoTL," as Niamh describes her journey from one research paradigm to another (Kelly, Nesbit, and Oliver 2012). As she wondered if others were on a similar journey, she met Susan Nesbit, from engineering, and Carolyn Oliver, from social work. The three formed a small, significant network in which they explored the nature of the STEM to SoTL journey. Through conference presentations and other conversations, Kelly and colleagues discovered like-minded colleagues from other institutions expanding their work to become inter-institutional. Niamh was a hub in this activity. From this perspective, she became increasingly involved in university-wide efforts to support SoTL. In so doing, she has become an emergent leader.

New Directions for Teaching and Learning • DOI: 10.1002/tl

Appointed Leadership in Support of Small SoTL Networks. Appointed leaders have the explicit responsibility for supporting teaching and learning within a unit or institution. They might be directors of teaching and learning centers or institutes for SoTL; associate deans or directors within faculties, schools, or departments; or chairs of teaching and learning committees. Whatever the formal position, it comes with the expectation that the person will help make teaching and learning better.

We propose, as an extension to the Williams and colleagues (2013) model, that making teaching and learning better can be achieved, in part, through the support of small significant networks. These networks may have come into existence independent of any efforts by the appointed leader. Appointed leaders with a good knowledge of the larger micro-level landscape can do hub-like work, helping small networks form valuable connections. This can be done informally as an institutional match-making exercise, or more formally by bringing networks together for events such as learning conferences or research seminars.

Another formal strategy used by appointed leaders to support SoTL is the implementation of skill-development workshops. Small networks often lack a broad repertoire of research methods or knowledge of SoTL literature. Appointed leaders address this need with formally structured events and programs. One such program is the International Leadership for the Scholarship of Teaching and Learning Program at UBC (Hubball, Clarke, and Poole 2010). Participants design research projects while learning about educational theories, research methods, and ways of going public with their work. They also form small networks within the program.

Appointed leaders must know their institutional landscape, and they must help create it. They need to know who the hubs are in order to adequately encourage and support them. Furthermore, the work of appointed leaders is only as good as the support received from the macro level. If senior administration decides that initiatives like the SoTL leadership program do not have value, meso-level local leaders are severely limited. Indeed, activity at all levels, from micro to macro, requires a valuing of quality teaching and learning and a belief that a scholarly approach to these is wise.

For example, Gary Poole's role as associate director of the School of Population and Public Health (SPPH) makes him an appointed leader. In fulfilling his mandate to support teaching and learning within SPPH, he relies considerably on emergent leaders. These are colleagues who form small networks to champion teaching innovation and SoTL research. Poole invites them to collaborate in workshops and retreats and links them with other colleagues who share these passions. Furthermore, he regularly asks them what they need in order to keep these networks thriving. It is worth noting that emergent leaders do not always self-identify. Rather, they are identified by the group (Hogg 2001). Because of this, one of the jobs of appointed leaders is to acknowledge the roles of their emergent colleagues. When appointed leaders at the meso or macro levels pay meaningful

NEW DIRECTIONS FOR TEACHING AND LEARNING • DOI: 10.1002/tl

attention to emergent leaders at the micro level, the appointed leaders are not micro managing, they are micro nurturing.

Paying attention to emergent leaders at the micro level also takes the form of mentoring graduate students (or developing leaders), many of whom are positioned to become future faculty or to take on leadership roles through staff positions within postsecondary institutions. We believe that it is essential for appointed leaders to embrace the values of generosity and service in their day-to-day activities in order to see mentoring as part of their role, particularly as it pertains to SoTL.

As a PhD student working in a staff position at the UBC Centre for Teaching Learning and Technology, opportunities to be mentored by appointed leaders are essential for connecting Roselynn Verwoord to small significant networks interested in SoTL as well as for helping her form valuable connections to emergent leaders championing SoTL at UBC. For Verwoord, being mentored by appointed leaders has immersed her in SoTL, an opportunity that she would not have had if appointed leaders had not embraced the values of generosity and service—values that are essential to mentoring developing leaders in SoTL. Verwoord's exposure to SoTL has shaped her future career interests and helped her develop important dyadic relationships with appointed leaders. These dyadic relationships have led to a number of meaningful collaborations existing within and beyond her CV. Despite the power difference inherent in these dyadic relationships, Verwoord has found that being aware of and discussing this power difference has helped to ensure that mentoring and paying attention have not become a process of "taking over."

Through case studies involving individuals in various emergent and appointed leadership positions at meso and micro levels at UBC, and through reflection on the development of our significant networks from our positions as appointed leader and developing leader at UBC, we have articulated how institutions can foster cultural change to support SoTL. By examining the nature of social networks in SoTL, relationships between these networks, and support for them, we have expanded on the role of social networks in SoTL (Roxå and Mårtensson 2009, 2012; Williams et al. 2013) in support of the institutional embedding of SoTL.

Conclusion

We believe that SoTL needs the kinds of social network analysis Roxå and Mårtensson (2009, 2012) have initiated not only to chart the nature of the connections but also to understand the content of communication within and between networks. Roxå and Mårtensson (2009, 2012) speculate that conversations within small networks are more effective if they are informed by scholarship and are about contributing to that scholarship. With this in mind, and applying our model, we need additional research to ascertain the following:

- How can emergent SoTL leaders be identified and nurtured at the small, significant network level?
- What are the most effective methods for appointed leaders working at the meso level to infuse scholarship into small network discussions?
- Can we find evidence for the hypothesized link between the scholarly nature of small network conversations and the quality of resultant teaching and learning?

These questions require research methods that involve the navigation of cause–effect terrain, which can be challenging to navigate because of the number of factors that intervene between a cause and an effect. Finally, what does our expanded model tell us about the best ways to weave SoTL into an institution's culture? SoTL training programs, along with events offered by teaching and learning centers and institutes for SoTL, have been established at many institutions across Canada (Poole and Simmons 2013). Their work is essential to the continued development of SoTL (Poole, Taylor, and Thompson 2007). Concurrently, the work of Williams and colleagues (2013), along with Roxå and Mårtensson's (2009, 2012) notion of small significant networks, establishes that comprehensive weaving of SoTL into institutional cultures requires numerous dyadic conversations that shed light on work being conducted at the front lines. These conversations take time; however, when meso-level appointed leaders pay attention to micro-level emergent leaders, hubs, and networks, we believe SoTL is much more likely to thrive.

Acknowledgments

Thank you to Andrea Williams, Terry Beery, Helen Dalton, James McKinnon, Jessica Pace, and Karen Strickland for their original contributions (cited in Williams et al. 2013), which this paper builds on. The authors, along with the above-named individuals, came together in 2011 through the International Collaborative Writing Groups of the International Society for the Scholarship of Teaching and Learning and articulated a multilevel model for embedding SoTL institutionally.

References

Burt, Ronald S. 2000. "The Network Structure of Social Capital." *Research in Organizational Behaviour* 22: 345–423.
Dawson, Shane, Jennifer Pei Ling Tan, and Erica McWilliam. 2011. "Measuring Creative Potential: Using Social Network Analysis to Monitor a Learners' Creative Capacity." *Australasian Journal of Educational Technology* 27(6): 924–942.
Hogan, Joyce, and Robert Hogan. 2002. "Leadership and Sociopolitical Intelligence." In *Multiple Intelligences and Leadership*, edited by Ronald E. Riggio, Susan E. Murphy, and Francis J. Pirozzolo, 76–89. Mahwah, NJ: Lawrence Erlbaum and Associates.

Hogg, Michael A. 2001. "A Social Identity Theory of Leadership." *Personality and Social Psychology Review* 5(3): 184–200.

Hubball, Harry T., Anthony Clarke, and Gary Poole. 2010. "Ten-year Reflections on Mentoring SoTL Research in a Research-Intensive University." *International Journal for Academic Development* 15(2): 117–129.

Kelly, Niamh, Susan Nesbit, and Carolyn Oliver. 2012. "A Difficult Journey: Transitioning from STEM to SoTL." *International Journal for the Scholarship of Teaching and Learning* 6 (1): Article 18.

Mårtensson, Katarina. 2014. "Influencing Teaching and Learning Microcultures. Academic Development in a Research-Intensive University." PhD diss., Lund University, Sweden.

Poole, Gary, Lynn Taylor, and John Thompson, J. 2007. "Using the Scholarship of Teaching and Learning at Disciplinary, National and Institutional Levels to Strategically Improve the Quality of Post-secondary Education" (Invited Essay). *International Journal of the Scholarship of Teaching and Learning* 1(2): 1–16.

Poole, Gary, and Nicola Simmons. 2013. "Contributions of the Scholarship of Teaching and Learning to Quality Enhancement in Canada." In *Enhancing Quality in Higher Education: International Perspectives*, edited by Ray Land and George Gordon, 118–128. London: Routledge.

Roxå, Torgny, and Katarina Mårtensson. 2009. "Significant Conversations and Significant Networks Exploring the Backstage of the Teaching Arena." *Studies in Higher Education* 34(5): 547–559.

Roxå, Torgny, and Katarina Mårtensson. 2012. "How Effects from Teacher Training of Academic Teachers Propagate into the Meso Level and Beyond." In *Teacher Development in Higher Education: Existing Programs, Program Impact, and Future Trends*, edited by Eszter Simon and Gabriela Pleschova, 213–233. London: Routledge.

Williams, Andrea, Roselynn Verwoord, Terry Beery, Helen Dalton, James McKinnon, Jessica Pace, Gary Poole, and Karen Strickland. 2013. "The Power of Social Networks: A Model for Weaving the Scholarship of Teaching and Learning into Institutional Culture." *Teaching and Learning Inquiry* 1(2): 49–62.

ROSELYNN VERWOORD *is a PhD student in the Department of Educational Studies at the University of British Columbia.*

GARY POOLE *is the past associate director of the School of Population and Public Health and current senior scholar in the Centre for Health Education Scholarship at the University of British Columbia.*

NEW DIRECTIONS FOR TEACHING AND LEARNING • DOI: 10.1002/tl

10

This chapter examines how SoTL has been integrated and supported at the University of Guelph based on three catalysts: (1) leadership commitment, (2) reward and recognition, and (3) integrated networks for sustained development.

Building Sustained Action: Supporting an Institutional Practice of SoTL at the University of Guelph

Natasha Kenny, Gavan P. L. Watson, Serge Desmarais

A cultural shift is occurring in higher education as institutions place growing emphasis on the importance of teaching and learning and support for faculty members who engage in the scholarship of teaching and learning (SoTL) (Schwartz and Haynie 2013). This shift in culture is largely grounded in changes to the norms, values, and shared assumptions that members of an academic community hold (Roxå, Mårtensson, and Alveteg 2011). Accounting for how these shifts in organizational culture occur, especially within the context of higher education, is inherently complex.

Using the University of Guelph, Ontario, as a case study, we will explore how SoTL has been integrated into the institution's teaching and learning culture. Drawing upon literature related to organizational change, especially within the context of higher education (for example, Bolden, Petrov, and Gosling 2008; Hannah and Lester 2009; Lakomski 2001; Roxå, Mårtensson, and Alveteg 2011; Trowler, Fanghanel, and Wareham 2005), we frame our case study around three key catalysts: (1) leadership commitment, (2) reward recognition, and (3) integrated networks.

Catalyst One: Leadership Commitment

Hannah and Lester (2009) and Bolden, Petrov, and Gosling (2008) acknowledge the tensions that exist in sustaining a balance among top-down, bottom-up, and lateral change processes. Despite these tensions, they highlight the importance of senior organizational leadership in catalyzing

New Directions for Teaching and Learning, no. 146, Summer 2016 © 2016 Wiley Periodicals, Inc.
Published online in Wiley Online Library (wileyonlinelibrary.com) • DOI: 10.1002/tl.20191

and supporting change by articulating a compelling vision; communicating the importance of making a shift; setting explicit guidelines for success; and providing appropriate financial, structural, strategic, and procedural resources. O'Meara (2006) further emphasizes the role of senior leadership in establishing cultural norms, structures, and processes to support engagement in multiple forms of scholarship, including SoTL.

Since 2005, the University of Guelph has been engaged in a sustained cultural shift and transformation in its undergraduate curriculum. The then university provost and vice president (academic), Maureen Mancuso, released "The Lighting of a Fire: Re-Imagining the Undergraduate Learning Experience," which challenged the university community to reimagine how it "structures and manifests" the undergraduate learning experience. In response to the white paper, the Office of the Associate Vice President Academic engaged in a series of consultations across the university community, and in 2007, it released the "Final Report of the Twenty-First Century (21C) Curriculum Committee," which contained a number of recommendations to foster curriculum change and operationalize the initiatives outlined in the white paper. Through these processes, the university's executive leadership demonstrated a strong vision for change.

In 2010, the Council of Ontario Universities (COU) released the Quality Assurance Framework. Senior leadership at Guelph committed to ensuring that quality assurance processes are viewed from a lens of continuous *quality enhancement* (Biggs, 2001). In keeping with this emphasis, SoTL has provided a vehicle to engage departments in a cycle of systematic dialogue, inquiry, and dissemination related to the quality of their academic programs. For example, many departments have presented their quality assurance processes and results at scholarly conferences, such as COU's annual Learning Outcomes Symposium. Like Hutchings, Huber, and Ciccone (2011), we see further potential for using SoTL to inform and complement program review and quality assurance processes.

University leaders have been modeling SoTL in their own work. Former University of Guelph president Alastair Summerlee has called on other institutions to further support SoTL (Charbonneau 2005). Many university leaders have directly engaged in SoTL (for example, Christensen Hughes and Mighty 2010; Mancuso et al. 2010; Murray and Summerlee 2007; Summerlee 2010a, 2010b; Summerlee and Christensen Hughes 2010; Summerlee and Murray 2010), communicating a clear statement of support through their own direct engagement in SoTL.

Senior leadership's commitment to fostering an institutional culture grounded in a commitment to continuous improvement has been paramount to fostering SoTL, which has emerged as a vehicle for improving teaching and learning practices. For example, the results of Mancuso, Desmarais, Parkinson, and Pettigrew (2010) influenced strategic curriculum initiatives to improve student engagement, such as the establishment of an expanded first-year seminar program, an increased number of intensive capstone experiences, and the creation of five institution-level learning outcomes. Further evidence of the impact of changes, such as the first-year seminar program, has been substantiated by SoTL (Summerlee and Murray 2010). Like Trigwell (2013), we see further opportunities to evidence the impact and purpose of SoTL, especially as it relates to improving student learning.

Catalyst Two: Reward and Recognition

Many authors highlight the challenges associated with the recognition of SoTL within faculty reward systems (Chalmers 2011; Hutchings, Huber, and Ciccone 2011; O'Meara 2005, 2006; Summerlee 2010b). Guelph has a flexible distribution of effort (DOE) structure that supports faculty members who are engaged in SoTL. All faculty members have a tripartite DOE (teaching, research, and service), that can be flexibly applied. An increasing number of faculty members have either been explicitly hired to engage in SoTL or have opted to engage in SoTL instead of, or concurrently with, their disciplinary research. Most deans and chairs have supported this shift, and positive evaluations of SoTL have also been evidenced through biannual promotion and tenure reviews. The recognition of SoTL in promotion and tenure has further fostered disciplinary and departmental cultures that value multiple forms of scholarship. Like Williams and others (2013), we highlight the importance of providing opportunities to incorporate SoTL into the DOE expectations for new faculty.

Awards and grants remain primary mechanisms for encouraging engagement in SoTL, providing resources and prestige to those who engage in SoTL (Chalmers 2011; Williams et al. 2013). Targeted SoTL grants provide an opportunity to support institutional strategic planning processes. In 2006, the University of Guelph established the Learning Enhancement Fund, which provides annual grants of up to $50,000 each to support projects that are designed to enhance student learning. Projects must align with integrated planning priorities, be grounded in scholarly literature, and include a plan of assessment. These awards have greatly enhanced the institution's ability to achieve and provide evidence of its strategic teaching and learning priorities. The university has also committed funding for instructor engagement in SoTL through its annual SoTL Faculty Fund (up to $12,000), Graduate Student SoTL Fund ($500), and the Provost's Study and Development Fellowships for Sessional Lecturers.

Catalyst Three: Integrated Networks for Sustained Development

Research has focussed on the importance of taking an integrated, multilevel approach to supporting organizational change (Bolden, Petrov, and Gosling 2008; Boyce 2003; Hannah and Lester 2009; Roxå and Mårtensson 2009; Roxå, Mårtensson, and Alveteg 2011; Trowler, Fanghanel, and

Wareham 2005; Williams et al. 2013). It is important to acknowledge that support for SoTL occurs throughout multiple levels within an academic institution. These levels can be conceptualized from the implementation of larger organization processes, structures, systems, and policies (macro level), to the formation of integrated disciplinary and cross-disciplinary social networks and working groups (meso level), to the development of individual SoTL practitioners and leaders (micro level) (Hannah and Lester 2009; Williams et al. 2013).

It is typical for organizations to focus on change at the institutional and individual levels (Bolden, Petrov, and Gosling 2008; Trowler, Fanghanel, and Wareham 2005). Institutional policies and reward structures may be established to promote and support strategic change. Targeted programs and initiatives may be implemented to develop individual knowledge catalysts to become leaders and champions who foster the dissemination of knowledge (Hannah and Lester 2009); however, establishing a culture of engagement in SoTL cannot rely on individual practitioners operating in isolation (Williams et al. 2013). Trowler and others (2005) and Bolden and others (2008) note the importance and challenge of establishing and sustaining social networks of support at the meso level. Here, educational development units provide a critical focus in bringing people together by linking social groups and networks of practice (Bolden, Petrov, and Gosling 2008; Roxå and Mårtensson 2009; Roxå, Mårtensson, and Alveteg 2011). These networks and groups engage in meaning-making and form micro cultures that actively influence decision-making processes, as well as prompt action and change (Hannah and Lester 2009; Mårtensson, Roxå, and Stensaker 2012).

The University of Guelph's educational development unit has created opportunities to link networks of practice. For over 25 years, the university's annual Teaching and Learning Innovations Conference has provided a forum for SoTL practitioners to disseminate knowledge related to their classroom experiences and wisdom of practice (Weimer 2001). In 2012, the institution launched a peer-reviewed publication, *Teaching and Learning Innovations*, providing an open-access space for disseminating SoTL. Williams and others (2013) speak to the importance of internal conferences and publications in helping to build networks and to support cultural norms related to teaching and learning. These links provide points of convergence between disciplinary cultures, where new ideas are inspired and teaching and learning norms and practices are further developed (Killen and Gallagher 2013; Roxå, Mårtensson, and Alveteg 2011).

In 2012, the university launched two faculty certificate programs that have helped build the expertise of individual SoTL practitioners and have further developed cross-disciplinary ties. Aligned with Roxå and others' (2011) academic network theory, many participants from the program have gone on to form their own disciplinary SoTL networks of practice, as evidenced by Bradley and others (2013). Another such initiative is highlighted through the College of Physical and Engineering Science's Physical Science and Engineering Education Research (PSEER) Centre, which provides funding and direct support for engagement in research related to teaching and learning. Other colleges across the institution are now looking to the PSEER as a model for promoting and sustaining disciplinary SoTL networks of practice for their faculty.

The institution has also committed to providing strong networks of SoTL practice at the graduate-student level. In 2013, the university approved the development of an inquiry-based graduate-student teaching certificate in SoTL, and each fall it offers a 12-week, cross-disciplinary, for-credit course in university teaching theory and practice. In order to encourage a strong institutional culture for SoTL, multiple authors (Gale and Golde 2004; Gurung et al. 2008; Kreber 2001) have written about the importance of integrating SoTL into graduate-student development programs. Like Williams and others (2013), Hutchings, Huber, and Ciccone (2011), Schwartz and Haynie (2013), Hutchings and others (2011), and Christensen Hughes and Mighty (2010), we note that educational development programs and initiatives as highlighted previously have played a critical role in creating and sustaining integrated SoTL networks across the institution.

Framing Our Case

As Poole, Taylor, and Thompson (2007) advocate, we suggest that value of and support for SoTL at the University of Guelph have been enhanced because SoTL has been aligned with institutional goals. We see both individuals and networks of practice across the institution use SoTL's cycle of systematic inquiry and dissemination to establish, implement, and investigate teaching and learning initiatives that support the institution's teaching and learning priorities. In turn, these acts each work to establish a reciprocal culture of teaching and learning that is supported by SoTL and a SoTL culture that is supported by the institution's culture for teaching and learning (see Figure 10.1).

Our three catalysts for supporting cultural shifts and support for SoTL occur at multiple levels throughout the institution. At the macro level, leadership commitment is essential for establishing a culture of continuous improvement, providing necessary organizational processes, strategic directions, and resources to catalyze and sustain change. At the meso level, educational development centers can support integrated networks for sustained development by establishing social links that bridge disciplinary lines. Here, it is of the utmost importance to provide opportunities for individuals and social groups from all disciplines to interact and share knowledge to build capacity related to their engagement in SoTL. Finally, support for engagement at the micro level through reward and recognition is most clearly encouraged through tangible incentives that legitimize SoTL in currently

Figure 10.1. Framework for Supporting SoTL at the University of Guelph

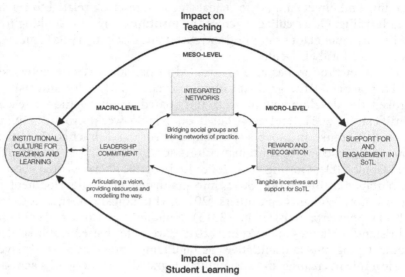

established faculty reward systems. Quite simply stated, support at this level follows a common tenet in higher education: "What gets rewarded gets done." In terms of monetary incentives, we note that targeted institutional grants for SoTL provide an opportunity to align with institutional strategic planning processes and thus, more broadly, enhance an institutional culture for teaching and learning.

Through a number of institutional-level initiatives, the University of Guelph established a strong value for and commitment to advancing their leadership in teaching and learning, which in turn was instrumental to supporting SoTL. With these networks established, the work now turns to sustaining momentum and evidencing whether engagement in SoTL has met its intended purposes (Trigwell 2013).

References

Biggs, John. 2001. "The Reflective Institution: Assuring and Enhancing the Quality of Teaching and Learning." *Higher Education* 41: 221–238.

Bolden, Richard, Georgy Petrov, and Jonathan Gosling. 2008. "Tensions in Higher Education Leadership: Towards a Multi-Level Model of Leadership Practice." *Higher Education Quarterly* 62(4): 358–376.

Boyce, Mary E. 2003. "Organizational Learning Is Essential to Achieving and Sustaining Change in Higher Education." *Innovative Higher Education* 28(2): 119–136. doi:10.1023/B:IHIE.0000006287.69207.00.

Bradley, Nicolette, Lorraine Jadeski, Genevieve Newton, Kerry Ritchie, Scott Merrett, and William Bettger. 2013. "The Use of a D2L Website to Serve as the Central Hub of a Network for the Scholarship of Teaching and Learning (SoTL) in an Academic Department." *Teaching and Learning Innovations* 15: 1–16.

Chalmers, Denise. 2011. "Progress and Challenges to the Recognition and Reward of the Scholarship of Teaching in Higher Education." *Higher Education Research & Development* 30(1): 25–38. doi:10.1080/07294360.2011.536970.

Charbonneau, Léo. 2005. "Scholarship of Teaching and Learning Comes of Age." *University Affairs*, 1–3.

Christensen Hughes, Julia, and Joy Mighty. 2010. *Taking Stock: Research on Teaching and Learning in Higher Education*. Kingston, ON: McGill-Queen University Press.

Gale, Richard, and Golde, Chris, M. 2004. "Doctoral Education and the Scholarship of Teaching and Learning." *Peer Review* 6(3): 8–12.

Gurung, Regan A. R., Pamela I. Ansburg, Patricia A. Alexander, Natalie Kerr Lawrence, and David E. Johnson. 2008. "The State of the Scholarship of Teaching and Learning in Psychology." *Teaching of Psychology* 35(4): 249–261. doi:10.1080/00986280802374203.

Hannah, Sean T., and Paul B. Lester. 2009. "A Multilevel Approach to Building and Leading Learning Organizations." *The Leadership Quarterly* 20(1): 34–48. doi:10.1016/j.leaqua.2008.11.003.

Hutchings, Pat, Mary T. Huber, and Anthony Ciccone. 2011. "Getting There: An Integrative Vision of the Scholarship of Teaching and Learning." *International Journal for the Scholarship of Teaching and Learning* 5(1): Article 31.

Killen, Patricia O'Connell, and Eugene V. Gallagher. 2013. "Sketching the Contours of the Scholarship of Teaching and Learning in Theology and Religion." *Teaching Theology and Religion* 16(2): 107–124.

Kreber, Carolin. 2001. "The Scholarship of Teaching and Its Implementation in Faculty Development and Graduate Education." *New Directions for Teaching and Learning* 86: 79–88.

Lakomski, Gabriele. 2001. "Organizational Change, Leadership and Learning: Culture as Cognitive Process." *The International Journal of Educational Management* 15(2): 68–77.

Mancuso, Maureen, Serge Desmarais, Kelly Parkinson, and Brian Pettigrew. 2010. *Disappointment, Misunderstanding and Expectations: A Gap Analysis of NSSE, BCSSE and FSSE*. Toronto: HEQCO.

Mårtensson, Katarina, Torgny Roxå, and Bjørn Stensaker. 2012. "From Quality Assurance to Quality Practices: An Investigation of Strong Microcultures in Teaching and Learning." *Studies in Higher Education* 39(4): 534–545.

Murray, Jacqueline, and Alastair Summerlee. 2007. "The Impact of Problem-Based Learning in an Interdisciplinary First-Year Program on Student Learning Behaviour." *Canadian Journal of Higher Education* 37(3): 87–107.

O'Meara, Kerry Ann. 2006. "Encouraging Multiple Forms of Scholarship in Faculty Reward Systems: Have Academic Cultures Really Changed?" *New Directions for Institutional Research* 129: 77–95.

O'Meara, Kerry Ann. 2005. "Encouraging Multiple Forms of Scholarship in Faculty Reward Systems: Does It Make a Difference?" *Research in Higher Education* 46(5): 479–510.

Poole, Gary D., Lynn Taylor, and John Thompson. 2007. "Using the Scholarship of Teaching and Learning at Disciplinary, National and Institutional Levels to Strategically Improve the Quality of Post-secondary Education." *International Journal for the Scholarship of Teaching and Learning* 1(2): 1–16.

Roxå, Torgny, and Katarina Mårtensson. 2009. "Significant Conversations and Significant Networks—Exploring the Backstage of the Teaching Arena." *Studies in Higher Education* 34(5): 547–559. doi:10.1080/03075070802597200.

Roxå, Torgny, Katarina Mårtensson, and Mattias Alveteg. 2011. "Understanding and Influencing Teaching and Learning Cultures at University: A Network Approach." *Higher Education* 62(1): 99–111. doi:10.1007/s10734-010-9368-9.

Schwartz, Beth M., and Aeron Haynie. 2013. "Faculty Development Centers and the Role of SoTL." *New Directions for Teaching and Learning* 136: 101–111. doi:10.1002/tl.20079

Summerlee, Alastair J. S. 2010a. "Challenge of Engagement Inside and Outside the Classroom: The Future for Universities." In *From Information to Knowledge: From Knowledge to Wisdom*, edited by Erik De Corte and Jens Erik Fenstad, 67–78. London: Portland Press Limited.

Summerlee, Alastair J. S. 2010b. "Gazing into the Crystal Ball: Where Should the Veterinary Profession Go Next?" *Journal of Veterinary Medical Education* 37(4): 328–333.

Summerlee, Alastair J. S., and J. Christensen Hughes. 2010. "Pressures for Change and the Future of University Education." In *Taking Stock: Research on Teaching and Learning in Higher Education*, edited by Julia Christensen Hughes and Joy Mighty, 243–260. Montreal: McGill-Queen's University Press.

Summerlee, Alastair J. S., and Jacqueline Murray. 2010. "The Impact of Enquiry-Based Learning on Academic Performance and Student Engagement." *Canadian Journal of Higher Education* 40(2): 78–94.

Trigwell, Keith. 2013. "Evidence of the Impact of Scholarship of Teaching and Learning Purposes." *Teaching and Learning Inquiry: The ISSOTL Journal* 1(1): 95–105. doi:10.1353/iss.2013.0004.

Trowler, Paul, Joelle Fanghanel, and Terry Wareham. 2005. "Freeing the Chi of Change: The Higher Education Academy and Enhancing Teaching and Learning in Higher Education." *Studies in Higher Education* 30(4): 427–444.

Weimer, Maryellen. 2001. "Learning More from the Wisdom of Practice." *New Directions for Teaching and Learning* 86: 45–56. doi:10.1002/tl.15.

Williams, Andrea L., Roselynn Verwoord, Theresa A. Beery, Helen Dalton, James McKinnon, Karen Strickland, Jessica Pace, and Gary Poole. 2013. "The Power of Social Networks: A Model for Weaving the Scholarship of Teaching and Learning into Institutional Culture." *Teaching and Learning Inquiry: The ISSOTL Journal* 1(2): 49–62.

NATASHA KENNY *is director of the educational development unit in the Taylor Institute for Teaching and Learning at the University of Calgary.*

GAVAN P. L. WATSON *is the associate director, eLearning, in the Teaching Support Centre at Western University.*

SERGE DESMARAIS *is the associate vice president (academic), at the University of Guelph.*

11

This chapter draws on other authors' ideas in this issue, describing parallels and outlining distinctions toward a synthesized model for the development of SoTL initiatives at the institutional level and beyond.

Synthesizing SoTL Institutional Initiatives toward National Impact

Nicola Simmons

The institutional case studies in this volume have provided examples and evidence of the ways in which postsecondary institutions in Canada have developed and sustained programs around the Scholarship of Teaching and Learning (SoTL) that impact the institutional pedagogical climate. The various chapters outline practices, including evidence of impact, and discuss continuing challenges with this work. While each chapter presents a perspective on one institutional context, there are common themes amongst the authors' recommendations that both affirm what can be found in the literature and extend that thinking. In this synthesis chapter, I will outline the following parallels: the importance of considering context, particularly during times of institutional change; the use of a micro-meso-macro-mega framework to understand the importance of social networks; leadership roles; and the notion of a developmental perspective. I end with implications and provide a synthesized model for the development of SoTL initiatives at the institutional level and beyond.

Considering Context

Several chapters address the importance of carefully considering the local context for SoTL, echoing Felton's (2013, 123) reminder that "any measure of good practice must account for both the scholarly and the local context where that work is being done." While Felton is referring primarily to classroom SoTL work, the principle is key in considering this volume's illustrations of different institutions and their particular contexts, and it echoes Mårtensson, Roxå, and Olsson's (2011) assertion that for greatest impact, SoTL strategies must be aligned with the culture of the institution.

NEW DIRECTIONS FOR TEACHING AND LEARNING, no. 146, Summer 2016 © 2016 Wiley Periodicals, Inc.
Published online in Wiley Online Library (wileyonlinelibrary.com) • DOI: 10.1002/tl.20192

For example, Miller-Young and colleagues' chapter explains that, given their transition to becoming a university, Mount Royal University found it helpful to position SoTL as research and to keep it separate from the teaching and learning center. In a different context, Timmermans and Ellis found that their predominantly STEM (science, technology, engineering, and math) faculty at the University of Waterloo preferred concrete teaching strategies over engagement in "social science" research approaches on their teaching. The institutional conference was reenvisioned to focus on scholarly teaching (which they found to be more inclusive of diverse scholars) rather than more traditionally defined SoTL that required peer-reviewed publication. The conference also includes an attendee favorite: "Igniting Our Practice" sessions that highlight teaching tips from award-winning faculty. Similarly, at Simon Fraser University, Amundsen and colleagues do not ask faculty members to include a literature review in their SoTL proposals, noting many are unfamiliar with SoTL publications; instead, team members identify relevant literature once the proposal has been finalized. In addition, they find that emphasizing different ways of making results public, both formal and informal, suits their context, tying to Huber's (2009) reminder that high impact SoTL has often been "made public" through informal means.

Many of the chapters are written about SoTL initiatives during times of significant institutional change. For example, Mengel outlines how Renaissance College sustained SoTL through a period of initial growth, budget cut backs, and further consolidation. Marquis and Ahmad discuss how McMaster University reenvisioned the entire teaching and learning center to include more focus on SoTL, establishing research fellows to undertake SoTL work in collaboration with the center, and thus raising SoTL's profile on campus. Timmermans and Ellis show how staff changes at uWaterloo created the ideal opportunity to evaluate the context for SoTL work. In each instance, these significant changes were not treated as impediments but rather as opportunities for thoughtful planning for new directions for SoTL work.

These points are key reminders: What has worked very well at one institution may need to be adapted prior to implementation at another. Applying templates for SoTL initiatives may in fact jeopardize the uptake if the local context is not taken into account.

Micro-Meso-Macro-Mega Framework

Many authors in this issue have found it useful to think about SoTL impact at several levels using a micro-meso-macro-mega framework (Poole 2009; Poole and Simmons 2013; Williams et al. 2013). *Micro* typically refers to the level of the individual instructor, *meso* to the department level, *macro* to what happens at the institutional level, and *mega* to disciplinary or provincial and national levels. While Amundsen and colleagues prefer the terminology of individual, departmental, and institutional levels, it seems to be helpful to consider the various levels of SoTL impact. For example, Wuetherick and Yu used the micro-meso-macro framework as a lens for analyzing the results of their national study, which helped show that concerns about support are often focused on the meso (department) level, especially around how work is assessed, and the macro (institution) level, particularly whether SoTL is valued as "real" research.

Building on this, I wish to highlight several further themes that make use of the micro-meso-macro framework, specifically the importance of social networks, the role of leaders, and a developmental view on these levels.

Importance of Social Networks. Several chapters discuss the role of social networks in supporting and sustaining SoTL growth. While not all make explicit the connection to the micro-meso-macro-mega framework, they all pertain to what is going on at these levels to support SoTL. For example, Verwoord and Poole show how social networks operate at each level: Small personal networks (micro) are a strong influence on teaching, and these micro discussions are more likely if the overall culture (meso and macro) is seen to support SoTL.

Miller-Young and colleagues report that Mount Royal University's program drew significantly on research about learning communities that supported meso-level connections. Marquis and Ahmad also found that an emphasis on partnerships such that SoTL scholars become part of a team has had a positive effect on scholarship. Similarly, Kenny, Watson, and Desmarais point to the importance of social networks at the meso level; these assist in creating space for the discussion of work in progress. They also note the key role an educational development center can play in creating interdisciplinary networks, echoing Poole, Taylor, and Thompson's (2007, 6) assertion of the importance that "institutions need a central entity" to support SoTL work.

Amundsen and colleagues note that much SoTL focuses on the development of the individual and does not consider the socially situated nature of SoTL work. They work to support informal micro networks: Once proposals are finalized, SoTL researchers are asked to discuss their work with other colleagues either informally over coffee or as a department presentation; many of these continue as connections and sometimes collaborations.

Further, Timmermans and Ellis refer to a study by Britnell and colleagues (2010) that found that the majority of faculty members (75 percent) learn about teaching through conversations with colleagues rather than by researching their own teaching. This is an important consideration: Faculty who are not reading the literature may still be talking about teaching. As Kenny, Watson, and Desmarais note, SoTL engages "departments in a cycle of systematic dialogue, inquiry, and dissemination related to the quality of their academic programs". SoTL, framed broadly, can thus provide a space for conversations about teaching that should be happening but perhaps are not.

An additional point of importance is the way in which SoTL networks can serve as a form of mentorship and a means to engage students. Wuetherick and Yu's national study found that 94 percent of participants felt the quality of their students' learning has improved as a result of the participants' SoTL work, but SoTL can go beyond this for greater impact on students. Marquis and Ahmad show how engaging students as co-inquirers helps ensure relevance to student audiences; it also engages students in key conversations about teaching and learning.

Leadership Roles.   While SoTL work has mostly been undertaken by individual scholars (sometimes working in small teams), institutional leaders have vital roles to play. For example, Wuetherick and Yu found that participants in their national study tended to express concern about a lack of high-level leadership to champion SoTL at their institutions; Miller-Young and colleagues note that such support has been critical to the Mount Royal SoTL Institute's success.

Verwoord and Poole highlight examples of individuals in diverse leadership positions (both appointed and "emergent") at the micro, meso, and macro levels. They emphasize the key role meso-level leaders can play, especially when they work to find and support micro-level networks and their hubs. In addition, they note that leadership is required at the macro level to catalyze an institutional culture that fosters SoTL growth. Similarly, Kenny, Watson, and Desmarais found that senior organizational leaders are key to catalyzing and supporting change, especially around "cultural norms, structures and processes" that support academics in their SoTL work.

Further, leadership at meso and macro levels can support engagement in conversations regarding how SoTL is aligned with institutional goals around educational quality. Marquis and Ahmad detail how at McMaster University, an early decision was made to focus on large-scale projects that aligned with institutional goals, and that would therefore have the maximum impact on student learning across the institution. Mengel discusses how policy frameworks that support SoTL, especially around tenure and promotion criteria that recognize and give credence to SoTL, are critical to its success.

Mengel also notes the importance of financial support at the faculty level; without it, he says, SoTL may become a "stepchild of scholarly work". Incentives for SoTL work do more than provide financial support. As Kenny, Watson, and Desmarais point out, they also create legitimacy around SoTL work by using an existing system of academic currency. Wuetherick, Yu, and Greer point to a lack of that legitimacy at their institution, where SoTL is not currently tied to promotion and tenure, although they note that is beginning to shift.

In these ways, SoTL efforts at each level (micro, meso, and macro) would contribute to the levels above and below them (see, for example, Williams et al. 2013). Ideally, SoTL would not only align with institutional goals, but it would also contribute to these goals in an ongoing two-way conversation.

Developmental Perspective. Miller-Young and colleagues found that newer faculty tended to frame impact in individual terms, whereas those further along in their careers tended to frame impact as relating to "their departments, the institution, or their disciplines". Additionally, they found a faculty member's engagement with SoTL may vary in relation to his or her career stage as represented by length of time at the institution. This suggests that an area for future exploration would be to determine if different SoTL supports are required at different career levels. Further, SoTL faculty indicated they had originally become involved in SoTL to grow their scholarship; the positive impact on their teaching seemed to be an ancillary benefit. The authors suggest that SoTL programs could thus have a positive socializing influence on newcomers to the institution.

Summary

Throughout the chapters, one can see a shift in institutional cultures toward environments that foster a positive regard for the importance of teaching and learning and valuing thoughtful inquiry into how to improve it. Overall, the picture is one of many SoTL scholars doing good work, much in the way of macro- or institutional-level support in the form of grants, promotion and tenure documents, and supportive leadership. There is still a need for a focus on building supports and networks at the micro and meso levels. Further, it is clear that leadership at the meso and macro levels has a strong role to play in creating space for these networks. As Williams and colleagues (2013, 52) argue, "if departments are the places where barriers to change exist, they are also important loci for change."

Figure 11.1 emphasizes the multidirectional nature of impact factors, showing how the micro level builds through the meso toward an impact at the macro level, as well as how supports might flow downward from the top. Each of these factors is important as a contributor to creating contexts that value SoTL, and in doing so, they support quality enhancement in teaching and learning.

Implications

Poole and Simmons (2013) highlighted a need for assessing SoTL's impact on institutional quality. While the chapters in this volume contribute to that agenda, further research is required to investigate and substantiate the ways in which SoTL contributes to institutional-level improvements in educational quality. In short, there is a need for further studies to examine the specific ways in which supports at each level contribute to broader SoTL impact.

NEW DIRECTIONS FOR TEACHING AND LEARNING • DOI: 10.1002/tl

Figure 11.1. SoTL Spheres

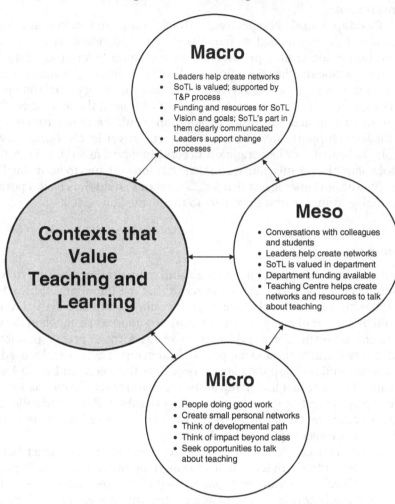

It also seems clear that if each level affects the one below and the one above, future research could explore to what extent that holds true once we move beyond the institution. That is, from where should advocacy for national frameworks for SoTL come? Is it primarily dependent on individual champions or are there opportunities for macro-level institutional impacts on national SoTL initiatives?

Further explorations of the developmental trend noted by Miller-Young and colleagues would also be interesting. As Andresen and Webb note, SoTL scholars can experience a shift in which

> instead of merely oneself ... one thinks in terms of the whole department, or maybe one's team of colleagues within it; then perhaps the School or Faculty;

then possibly the university ... then maybe a state or national conference on teaching and learning in one's subject area. (as cited in Trigwell, Martin, Benjamin, and Prosser 2000, 157)

If this is developmental growth, what would support movement toward a broader perspective? If SoTL scholars are finding themselves blocked at the meso level, what can be done to mitigate the barriers at this level so greater macro impact can be realized? And, if national advocacy, as Poole, Taylor, and Thompson (2007) identified, remains elusive, what will it take to put in place macro-level supports? Who will step forward to become the all-important hubs discussed in Verwoord and Poole's chapter?

Final Thoughts

The process for writing this volume was based on Healey and Marquis's (2013) model for the International Society for the Scholarship of Teaching and Learning's International Writing Groups. As we underwent our writing and collegial peer-review process (each of us read others' work in progress and provided feedback at two points), we became aware of the ways in which our process paralleled the recommendations for growing SoTL using a micro-meso-macro-mega framework. As individuals, we partnered with others in small significant micro networks to write these chapters. With minimal leadership, these partnerships came together to produce the volume you are now reading. The chapters, by outlining what happens at micro, meso, and macro levels, contribute to the mega level by providing an overview of the national SoTL landscape.

Returning to Poole, Taylor, and Thompson's (2007) recommendations (as outlined in Chapter 1 of this volume), arguably we have an infrastructure in place in the form of SoTL Canada. We have made our conversations public in this volume. We turn now to thoughts of greater advocacy. Applying our top-down/bottom-up model, we can ask what role SoTL Canada might play in creating alignment of its aims with institutional goals across the county. In what ways might SoTL Canada and its members serve as hubs to build toward the national infrastructure Poole, Taylor, and Thompson (2007) recommend?

Further experimentation will be needed to assess the extent to which the ideas in this volume can be implemented in other settings. At the same time, an ongoing challenge in postsecondary education is knowledge implementation: getting the good work into practice. It is our hope that colleagues will find useful the ideas and frameworks in this volume and will create ways to put them into practice in their own contexts. To follow Hutchings (2000), we hope these accounts of what has been done and what works have come together to contribute to theory building and to visions of the possible.

Acknowledgments

My warmest thanks to Lori Goff for being a sounding board during the writing of this chapter and to the many extraordinary colleagues who contributed chapters to the volume. You continue to be an outstanding and significant SoTL network.

References

Britnell, Judy, Bettina Brockerhoff-Macdonald, Lorraine Carter, Debra Dawson, Leslie Doucet, Frederick Evers, Shirley Hall, et al. 2010. *University Faculty Engagement in Teaching Development Activities Phase II*. Toronto: Higher Education Quality Council of Ontario.

Felton, Peter. 2013. "Principles of Good Practice in SoTL." *Teaching & Learning Inquiry* 1(1): 121–125.

Healey, Mick, and Beth Marquis. (Eds.). 2013. Writing Without Borders: 2013 International Writing Collaborative. *Teaching and Learning Inquiry* 1(2): 3–8.

Huber, Mary Taylor. 2009. "Teaching Travels: Reflections on the Social Life of Classroom Inquiry and Innovation." *International Journal for the Scholarship of Teaching and Learning* 3(2), Article 2.

Hutchings, Pat. 2000. *Opening Lines: Approaches to the Scholarship of Teaching and Learning*. Palo Alto, CA: Carnegie Foundation for the Advancement of Teaching.

Mårtensson, Katerina, Torgny Roxå, and Thomas Olsson. 2012. "Developing a Quality Culture through the Scholarship of Teaching and Learning." *Higher Education Research & Development*, 30(1): 51–62.

Poole, Gary. 2009, May 25–27. "The Pursuit of the Scholarship of Teaching and Learning in Canada: Good, but Not Good Enough." Keynote presentation at the Annual Canadian Society for Studies in Higher Education Conference, Ottawa, ON.

Poole, Gary, and Nicola Simmons. 2013. "The Contributions of the Scholarship of Teaching and Learning to Quality Enhancement in Canada." In *Quality Enhancement in Higher Education: International Perspectives*, edited by George Gordon and Ray Land, 118–128. London: Routledge.

Poole, Gary, Lynn Taylor, and John Thompson. 2007. "Using the Scholarship of Teaching and Learning at Disciplinary, National and Institutional Levels to Strategically Improve the Quality of Post-secondary Education." *International Journal for the Scholarship of Teaching and Learning* 1(2): 1–16.

Williams, Andrea, Roselynn Verwood, Theresa A. Beery, Helen Dalton, James McKinnon, Karen Strickland, Jessica Pace, and Gary Poole. 2013. "The Power of Social Networks: A Model for Weaving the Scholarship of Teaching and Learning into Institutional Culture." *Teaching and Learning Inquiry* 1(2): 49–62.

NICOLA SIMMONS *was the founding chair of SoTL Canada and is currently a faculty member in the faculty of education at Brock University in Ontario.*

INDEX

Advancing the Scholarship of Teaching and Learning, 14
Ahmad, A., 8, 47, 54, 96–98
Alan Blizzard Award, 41
Allin, L., 51
Alveteg, M., 87, 89, 90
Amundsen, C., 8, 31, 35, 38, 96, 97
Austin, A., 71

Baepler, P., 48, 49
Bass, R., 74
Bateman, D., 23
Beach, A., 71
Benjamin, J., 64, 101
Bennett, C., 55
Bernstein, D., 11
Bernstein, J. L., 47
Biggs, J., 88
Billett, S., 32, 36
Bishop, M., 39
Boadu, N. Y., 57
Boardman, C., 47
Bolden, R., 87, 89, 90
Boyce, M. E., 89
Boyer, E., 13, 14, 37
Bradley, N., 90
Brame, C., 58
Brent, R., 74
Drew, A., 18
Britnell, J., 73, 97
Brook, P., 31
Burt, R. S., 82

Canada: higher education, SoTL in, 23–24, 28–29; current study, 24; teaching commons, 24–28; history of SoTL in, 13, 19–21; Canadian context, 14; development of, 17–19; early days, 14–17; origins of, 13–14
The Canadian Journal for the Scholarship of Teaching and Learning (CJ SoTL), 17
Carey, M., 9, 55, 62
Carnegie Academy, 55
Carnegie Academy for Scholarship of Teaching and Learning (CASTL), 24
Carpenter-Hubin, J., 41
Carr, M., 39

CASTL. *See* Carnegie Academy for Scholarship of Teaching and Learning (CASTL)
Centeno, A., 31
Centra, J. A., 37
Centre for Leadership in Learning (CLL), 47
Centre for Teaching Excellence (CTE), 72
Chalmers, D., 89
Charbonneau, L., 17, 88
Chick, N., 12
Chick, N. L., 58
Christensen Hughes, J., 7, 15, 16, 88, 91
Ciccone, A., 14, 63, 64, 67–69, 88, 89, 91
Ciccone, T., 29
CJ SoTL. See The Canadian Journal for the Scholarship of Teaching and Learning (CJ SoTL)
Clarke, A., 47, 83
Clarke, D., 32, 35, 36
Clarke, G., 39
CLL. *See* Centre for Leadership in Learning (CLL)
Cohen, B., 48, 49
Colford, J. A., 39
Collins, J. C., 41
Communities of practice (CoPs), 80
Conway, K., 55
CoPs. *See* Communities of practice (CoPs)
Corley, E. A., 47
COU. *See* Council of Ontario Universities (COU)
Council of Ontario Universities (COU), 88
Couturier, C., 40–42
Cox, M. D., 55
Craig, C. M., 29
CTE. *See* Centre for Teaching Excellence (CTE)

Dalton, H., 85
Dan, B., 12
Dawson, D., 17
Dawson, S., 82
Dawson, T., 15

Desmarais, S., 9, 87, 88, 94, 97, 98
Dewar, J., 55
Distribution of effort (DOE), 89
DOE. *See* Distribution of effort (DOE)
Dolmans, D., 31

ED. *See* Educational development (ED)
Eddy, P., 71
Educational development (ED), 19
Educational research associate (ERA), 74
Ellis, D., 73
Ellis, D. E., 9, 60, 71, 78
Elton, L., 29
Emergent leadership, for SoTL networks, 82. *See also* Scholarship of Teaching and Learning (SoTL)
Emmioglu, E., 8, 31, 35, 38
ERA. *See* Educational research associate (ERA)
Evans, B., 55

Fanghanel, J., 87, 89, 90
Felder, R. M., 74
Felten, P., 50, 51
Felton, P., 95
Force, K., 19

Gale, R., 56, 91
Gallagher, E. V., 90
Gelula, M., 31
Gijbels, D., 31
Ginsberg, S. M., 47
Gladwell, M., 20
Glassick, C. E., 64
Golde, Chris, M., 91
Gosling, J., 87, 89, 90
Greer, J., 9, 63, 70, 98
Gurung, R. A. R., 91

Halliwell, J., 15
Hannah, S. T., 87, 89, 90
Haynie, A., 87, 91
Healey, M., 101
HEQCO. *See* Higher Education Quality Council of Ontario (HEQCO)
Higginbottom, G. M. A., 57
Higher Education Quality Council of Ontario (HEQCO), 16, 73
Hoffman, S., 55
Hogan, J., 82
Hogan, R., 82

Hogg, M. A., 83
Hollingsworth, H., 32, 35, 36
Hotton, V., 8, 31, 38
Hubball, H., 14, 47
Hubball, H. T., 83
Huber, M., 23, 24, 29, 63, 64, 66–69
Huber, M. T., 14, 88, 89, 91, 96
Hum, G., 8, 31, 35, 38
Hunt, G., 16
Hutchings, P., 14, 23, 24, 29, 63, 64, 66–69, 74, 88, 89, 91, 101

Integrators, 40
International Society for the Scholarship of Teaching and Learning (ISSoTL), 14
ISSoTL. *See* International Society for the Scholarship of Teaching and Learning (ISSoTL)

Kelly, N., 82
Kember, D., 55
Kenny, N., 9, 87, 94, 97, 98
Killen, Patricia O'Connell, 90
Kindler, A., 15
Knoblauch, H., 57
Kreber, C., 31, 37, 91
Kunz, D., 55
Kuruganti, U., 40, 41
Kwo, O., 23, 29

Lakomski, G., 87
Learning, 13
Learning Enhancement Fund, 89
Learning Innovation and Teaching Enhancement (LITE) Grants, 74–75
Lester, P. B., 87, 89, 90
Likert-scale questions, 58
LITE Grants. *See* Learning Innovation and Teaching Enhancement (LITE) Grants

Maeroff, G. I., 64
Maki, P., 37
Manarin, K., 9, 55, 62
Mancuso, M., 88
Mann, K., 31
Marquis, B., 101
Marquis, E., 8, 47, 48, 54
Martensson, K., 29
Mårtensson, K., 49, 79, 81, 82, 84, 85, 87, 89, 90, 95

Martin, E., 64, 101
Mather, J., 16
McDougall, P., 64
McKinney, K., 7, 13, 50, 63, 66
McKinnon, J., 85
McMaster Institute for Innovation and Excellence in Teaching and Learning (MIIETL), 47–48; SoTL at; developing priority areas for, 52; engaging students, 50–52; establishment of, 48–50
McWilliam, E., 82
Meadows, K., 16, 17
Mengel, T., 8, 39–42, 45, 96, 98
Mighty, J., 7, 16, 48, 88, 91
MIIETL. See McMaster Institute for Innovation and Excellence in Teaching and Learning (MIIETL)
Miller-Young, J., 9, 55, 62, 96–100
Min-Leliveld, M., 31
3M National Teaching Fellowship, 40
Mount Royal University (MRU), 55
Mount Royal University's Human Research Ethics Board, 58
MRU. See Mount Royal University (MRU)
Murray, J., 88, 89

Needham, T., 40, 43
Nesbit, S., 82
Neumann, A., 11, 12
Nexen Scholars Program, 55, 56
Norton, L. S., 35, 37

Oliver, C., 82
Olsson, T., 49, 95
O'Meara, K. A., 11, 88, 89
Ontario Ministry of Training, Colleges, and Universities, 50
Otis, M. M., 50

Pace, D., 63
Pace, J., 85
Parkinson, K., 88
Pedagogic resonance, 36
Petrov, G., 87, 89, 90
Pettigrew, B., 88
Physical Science and Engineering Education Research (PSEER), 91
Pillars, 14
Pillay, J. J., 57

Poole, G., 7–9, 13–16, 18, 20, 22–24, 34, 47, 52, 60, 79, 83, 85, 86, 96–99, 101
Poole, G. D., 91
Porras, J. I., 41
Pracht, C., 55
Prideaux, D., 31
Prosser, M., 64, 101
PSEER. See Physical Science and Engineering Education Research (PSEER)

RAs. See Research assistants (RAs)
RC. See Renaissance College (RC)
Rege Colet, N., 71
Renaissance College (RC), 39; SoTL at, 39–40, 43–44; academic plan, 42; teaching faculty, presentations and publications of, 40–41; UNB's task force, 42–43; vision, values, and purpose, 41–42
Research assistants (RAs), 33
Ritch, S., 42
Roxå, T., 49, 79, 81, 82, 84, 85, 87, 89, 90, 95

Scholarship of Teaching and Learning (SoTL), 13; in Canada; higher education, 23–29; history of, 13–21; goal of, 13; inquiring into the impact of inquiry: assessing impact, 57–58; background, 55–56; future work, 61; methods, 58–59; outcomes, 59–61; program description, 56–57; scholars program structure 2009–2013, 57; institutional initiatives toward national impact, 95–96; implications, 99–101; micro-meso-macro-mega framework, 96–99; intentional design of, 31–33; alignment of, 35–37; conducting the project, 34; ongoing improvement, 35; project development, 33–34; sharing findings, 34–35; at MIIETL, 47–53; moving forward, 19–21; origins of, 13–14; at Renaissance College, 39–44; small significant networks and leadership role in, 79; emergent and appointed leaders, 82–84; importance of dyadic interactions, 81–82; institutional cultures, 80; small significant networks and, 81; at the University of Guelph, 87–92; at the University of

Saskatchewan, 63–69; at the University of Waterloo, 71–77; *See also* Canada; McMaster Institute for Innovation and Excellence in Teaching and Learning (MIIETL); Renaissance College (RC); University of Guelph; University of Saskatchewan (U of S); University of Waterloo (UWaterloo)

SchÖnwetter, D., 23

School of Population and Public Health (SPPH), 83

Schroeder, C. M., 52

Schwartz, B. M., 87, 91

Science, Technology, Engineering, and Mathematics (STEM), 82

Shale, S., 36

Shulman, L., 14, 24, 64, 74

SIG. *See* Special interest group (SIG)

Simmons, N., 7–10, 13–16, 18, 22–24, 79, 85, 95, 96, 99, 102

Smentkowski, B., 55

Snowball sampling technique, 64

Social Sciences and Humanities Research Council, 15

Society of Teaching and Learning in Higher Education (STLHE), 13, 24

Sorcinelli, M. D., 71

SoTL. *See* Scholarship of Teaching and Learning (SoTL)

Special interest group (SIG), 18

Spencer, J., 31

SPPH. *See* School of Population and Public Health (SPPH)

Starrett, D., 55

Steinert, Y., 31

STEM. *See* Science, Technology, Engineering, and Mathematics (STEM)

Stensaker. B., 90

Stes, A., 31

Stewart, A. C., 41

STLHE. *See* Society of Teaching and Learning in Higher Education (STLHE)

Strickland, K., 85

Summerlee, A., 88

Summerlee, A. J. S., 88, 89

Taking Stock Symposium (2008), 16

Tan, J. P. L., 82

Taylor, B. A. P., 52

Taylor, K. L., 16, 18, 20, 23, 71

Taylor, L., 7, 14, 15, 17, 47, 52, 85, 91, 97, 101

Teaching and Learning Development Grants Program, 32

Terosky, A. L., 11

Theall, M., 37

Thomas, J., 42

Thompson, J., 7, 16, 18, 20, 23, 47, 52, 85, 91, 97, 101

Timmermans, J., 73

Timmermans, J. A., 9, 60, 71, 78

Tri-Council Agencies, 15

Trigwell, K., 36, 55, 64, 89, 92, 101

Trowler, P., 87, 89, 90

UBC. *See* University of British Columbia (UBC)

UNB. *See* University of New Brunswick's (UNB)

University of British Columbia (UBC), 79

University of Guelph, 87; framing case, 91–92; integrated networks for sustained development, 89–91; leadership commitment, 87–89; reward and recognition, 89

University of New Brunswick's (UNB), 39, 42–43. *See also* Renaissance College (RC)

University of Saskatchewan (U of S), 63–64; SoTL at, 63–64; barriers and challenges, 66–67; community, 65–66; supporting, 67–69

University of Waterloo (UWaterloo), 71; SoTL at, 71; annual teaching and learning conference, 76; catalysts, 72–73; contemplating impacts, 76–77; institutional context, 71–72; reconceptualization phase, 73–74; responding to the influences, 74–76

U of S. *See* University of Saskatchewan (U of S)

Urquhart, S., 68

UWaterloo. *See* University of Waterloo (UWaterloo)

Valk, J., 40, 41

Van Petegem, P., 31

Verwoord, R., 9, 34, 60, 79, 84, 86, 97, 98, 101

Walker, J. D., 48, 49
Wareham, T., 87, 90
Waterman, M., 55
Watson, G. P. L., 9, 87, 94, 97, 98
Weber, J., 55
Weimer, M., 90
Werder, C, 50
Williams, A., 24, 29, 79–85, 96, 98, 99
Williams, A. L., 60, 89–91
Wilsman, A., 58
Wilson, M., 31
Woodhouse, R., 19

Workplace learning, 36
Wuetherick, B., 8, 9, 17, 23, 30, 63, 70, 97, 98

Xin, C., 8, 31, 38

Yeo, M., 9, 55, 62
Yu, S., 7–9, 23, 30, 63, 70, 97, 98

Zimmer, J., 9, 55, 62
Zundel, P., 39–42
Zundel, P. E., 40, 41

NEW DIRECTIONS FOR TEACHING AND LEARNING
ORDER FORM SUBSCRIPTION AND SINGLE ISSUES

DISCOUNTED BACK ISSUES:

Use this form to receive 20% off all back issues of *New Directions for Teaching and Learning*.
All single issues priced at **$23.20** (normally $29.00)

TITLE   ISSUE NO.   ISBN

_____ _____ _____

_____ _____ _____

_____ _____ _____

*Call 1-800-835-6770 or see mailing instructions below. When calling, mention the promotional code JBNND to receive
your discount. For a complete list of issues, please visit www.wiley.com/WileyCDA/WileyTitle/productCd-TL.html*

SUBSCRIPTIONS: (1 YEAR, 4 ISSUES)

☐ New Order   ☐ Renewal

U.S.	☐ Individual: $89	☐ Institutional: $356
CANADA/MEXICO	☐ Individual: $89	☐ Institutional: $398
ALL OTHERS	☐ Individual: $113	☐ Institutional: $434

*Call 1-800-835-6770 or see mailing and pricing instructions below.
Online subscriptions are available at www.onlinelibrary.wiley.com*

ORDER TOTALS:

Issue / Subscription Amount: $ _____

Shipping Amount: $ _____
(for single issues only – subscription prices include shipping)

Total Amount: $ _____

SHIPPING CHARGES:

First Item $6.00
Each Add'l Item $2.00

*(No sales tax for U.S. subscriptions. Canadian residents, add GST for subscription orders. Individual rate subscriptions must
be paid by personal check or credit card. Individual rate subscriptions may not be resold as library copies.)*

BILLING & SHIPPING INFORMATION:

☐ **PAYMENT ENCLOSED:** *(U.S. check or money order only. All payments must be in U.S. dollars.)*

☐ **CREDIT CARD:** ☐ VISA   ☐ MC   ☐ AMEX

Card number _____Exp. Date_____

Card Holder Name_____Card Issue # _____

Signature _____Day Phone_____

☐ **BILL ME:** *(U.S. institutional orders only. Purchase order required.)*

Purchase order # _____
            Federal Tax ID 13559302 • GST 89102-8052

Name_____

Address_____

Phone_____ E-mail_____

Copy or detach page and send to: **John Wiley & Sons, Inc. / Jossey Bass**
                                   PO Box 55381
                                   Boston, MA 02205-9850

PROMO JBNND

Small changes that make a big difference

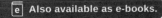

DATE DUE